HOW TO
LET GOD HELP
YOU

Additional books by Myrtle Fillmore

Wee Wisdom's Way—1894
  (No longer available)
Myrtle Fillmore's Healing Letters—1948
  (Edited by Frances W. Foulks; originally
  published as *Letters of Myrtle Fillmore*—
  1936)

Books by Charles Fillmore

Christian Healing—1909
Talks on Truth—1909
The Twelve Powers of Man—1930
Metaphysical Bible Dictionary—1931
Prosperity—1936
Mysteries of Genesis—1936
Jesus Christ Heals—1939
Teach Us to Pray—1941
  (Co-authored with Cora Dedrick Fillmore)
Mysteries of John—1946
Atom-Smashing Power of Mind—1949
Keep a True Lent—1953
The Revealing Word—1959
Dynamics for Living—1967
  (Edited by Warren Meyer)
The Charles Fillmore Concordance—1975
  (Compiled by Clinton Bernard)

Book by Cora Dedrick Fillmore

Christ Enthroned in Man—1937

All books are shown with their original publication dates.

How to Let God Help You

Myrtle Fillmore

Selected and arranged
by Warren Meyer

New Introduction
by Rosemary Fillmore Rhea

Unity Village, MO 64065

The painting on the cover is a computerized photo enhancement featuring Myrtle Fillmore's desk and personal mementos, courtesy of the Heritage Room at Unity Village, Missouri.

Cover design and photo enhancement by Chad Pio
Cover photograph by Gene King

How to Let God Help You
was first published in 1956.

Eleven printings through 1991
Paperback edition 1994

The American Standard Version used for
all Bible verses, unless otherwise noted.

LIBRARY OF CONGRESS CATALOGING-IN-PUBLICATION DATA

Fillmore, Myrtle, 1845-1931.
    How to Let God Help You; selected and arranged by Warren Meyer.
    p. cm.
    Includes index.
    1. Unity School of Christianity. 2. New Thought.
I. Meyer, Warren. II. Title.
BX9890.U506F55   1956
289.9'7—dc20   94-774
ISBN 0-87159-057-3. —ISBN 0-87159-185-5 (pbk.)
Canada GST R132529033

Unity Books feels a sacred trust to be a healing presence in the world. By printing with biodegradable soybean ink on recycled paper, we believe we are doing our part to be wise stewards of our Earth's resources.

INTRODUCTION TO THE 1994 EDITION

I'm writing this as I sit on a terrace overlooking the sea on the beautiful island of Saint Croix in the Virgin Islands. I have traveled here to speak to a group of people who have come together because they are interested in exploring the teachings of Unity. To me, it is remarkable that I'm here because long, long ago, on a spring night in 1889, a frail, sick woman walked into a lecture hall in Kansas City, Missouri, and came away with an idea that saved her life and eventually led her to health and wholeness. This idea was not to let her go until she and her husband, who was soon set afire with it too, had found a faith that reached around the world and blessed the lives of millions of people throughout this century.

Myrtle and Charles Fillmore became magnificently obsessed with the idea that if they committed themselves to the spirit of God within them, God would do the rest. They knew if they put God first, they would be healed, they would be prospered, and they would be free.

They dreamed of a healing ministry that would reach around the world to bless and inspire all people to move beyond their humanness into a conscious awareness of who they really are. They dreamed of a city of God, a "new Jerusalem," where people of all races, all religions would come and feel the presence of the Lord within them. And this dream became a reality because they had absolute faith that with God all things are possible.

Two sick, poverty-ridden people found a faith—made the quantum leap from darkness and despair into the light of all possibilities.

Myrtle Fillmore was my grandmother, and although she passed on to another dimension of living when I was quite young, she has been an inspiration to me throughout my life. Myrtle was truly an amazing woman. Although she was born into an era when few women went to college, she did and then became a schoolteacher. She left her home and family in Ohio and took a school in Clinton, Missouri. After a while, because of her failing health, she moved to Denison, Texas, and there met Charles Fillmore, a young railroad clerk. Charles and Myrtle were married in 1881. Together they went to Colorado where Charles sought his fortune in the real estate business. Two of their three sons were born there. After the real estate boom faded in Colorado, the Fillmore family moved to Kansas City, Missouri. In a modern mobile society, this might seem just the ordinary sequence of events. But for a refined lady of the nineteenth century, traveling across treacherous mountain passes in a horse-drawn carriage would have been considered quite unusual. Marrying an uneducated frontiersman and bearing two sons in a rough, dusty boomtown was hardly what one would have expected from a fragile, aesthetic woman. But Myrtle was not an ordinary person, and her spirit could never be confined by doing the expected. I think she always knew that if she trusted her soul's guidance, it would lead her to her spiritual destiny.

In a time when few women worked, Myrtle spent her days in the Unity offices, working side by side with her husband—praying, healing, creating Unity. She raised three wonderful sons. She created a magazine for children called *Wee Wisdom*, which spanned nearly a century of publication. Myrtle was a spiritually liberated woman who dedicated her life to helping people explore the wonder within them.

I wish that I could share with my grandmother the stories that people tell me of how Unity has changed their lives. My travels have taken me around the world, and in so many unexpected places, I have met people who read *Daily Word* magazine or pray with Silent Unity. These people are part of a network of prayer that reaches around the planet. A network that had its beginning with one woman's commitment to the healing power of God that was revealed to her that spring night in 1889.

As we move into the twenty-first century, I

know that Unity's mission in our world will be even more important. Why? Because it is a healing ministry. It looks beyond the theologies that separate into the love that inspired all religions. And because Unity has no strict doctrine or dogma to protect, it transcends the walls we have erected that keep us from experiencing our oneness with God.

Unity's mission in our world is to help people release those fears and hurts that bind and confine so that we may experience and express the love that we are.

This mystical, loving light that we call Unity is universal. It is that in us that sees beyond what seems to be, into what is real and true. It knows no special religion—it has no national boundary—no cultural division. It is the Unity that flows from the heart of the universe to heal and bless our world.

I have seen the spirit of Unity as I looked into the faces of Unity friends in Moscow; I saw it in the lovely eyes of a Polynesian woman who lives on a remote island in the South Pacific a thousand miles from Tahiti. It was in the smile of a Buddhist monk in Japan ... in the laughter of a young Hindu friend in New Delhi ... in the devotion of a Muslim family in Tehran, Iran. This Spirit is everywhere present. And, as we come together in this Spirit, we become a part of the evolution of the consciousness of love that will lift our world into the millennium.

And so, dear reader, as you study Myrtle Fillmore's *How to Let God Help You*, I pray that you will be inspired by Myrtle's love and faith as I have been. This is not just a book, it's more like a friend that will be there for you when you need to be reminded that you can never be separate from the loving Spirit that created you and all of life. God bless you on your way.

—Rosemary Fillmore Rhea
Prairie Village, Kansas
January 1994

FOREWORD

Although Myrtle Fillmore passed to the invisible side of life on October 6, 1931, the memories of her loving presence are still felt by all who knew and worked with her. She was a friend of those who needed her friendship. She was a counselor to those who sought her advice. She was a teacher to those who wanted to learn the Truth of Jesus Christ. She prayed with and for those who desired help. Many who sought her prayer blessings brought forth renewed bodies. Prosperity and success were gained by others who had faith in her teachings pertaining to the practical application of Truth. And there were those who found that prayer brought forth for them a new rightness as they lived and worked with others.

Myrtle Fillmore proved the Christ Truth in her own life and affairs. The healing, prospering, and harmonizing ideas of Divine Mind moved through her consciousness and inaugurated a glorious, unifying ministry of love. Today, through Unity School of Christianity with its periodicals, books, and booklets, and the many Unity centers throughout the world, this ministry continues and serves all who seek its inspiring and practical help.

The only book as such that Myrtle Fillmore wrote was *Wee Wisdom's Way*, which was an expression of her love for children and her interest in helping them understand God's wonderful Truth. Her desire to bless children with rich spiritual ideas flowered into *Wee Wisdom*, America's oldest magazine for children, of which she was editor for many years. Mrs. Fillmore seemed to stay in the background when it came to writing books, since her husband, Charles Fillmore, had such a great leaning in that direction of expressing Truth. However, she carried on a rich ministry through her healing and prayer letters. In 1936, Unity School published a book* composed of extracts from her letters, compiled by Frances W. Foulks.

The material used in this, her third book, came from three general sources. First, Myrtle Fillmore's letters were carefully searched and from them the finest expressions of her spiritual consciousness were taken. Second, a survey was made of the early Unity literature, from which were extracted many spiritually practical suggestions in columns written by her. Third, a sealed envelope was opened recently in which were found lectures that Mrs. Fillmore delivered in Chicago during the summer of 1890. (The chapters dealing with the basic principles of Truth came from these lesson-lectures.)

This book has been lovingly prepared with a two-fold purpose. It is designed to bring

Letters of Myrtle Fillmore, now called *Myrtle Fillmore's Healing Letters*

Unity readers and students everywhere the inspired thoughts of Myrtle Fillmore. In these writings she talks personally to all who seek the Jesus Christ Truth. She speaks as a friend to each reader. Also, this material is presented as a textbook so that a student may, if he chooses, study systematically the Unity teachings.

Charles and Myrtle Fillmore were the co-founders of Unity. Today, that which they started in faith is blessing the whole world. It is the prayer of Unity School that the wealth of spiritual thoughts which radiated from "Mama Myrtle" (her co-workers often called her lovingly by this name) and blessed so many in the past will once again heal the sick, supply the poor, and bring peace and harmony to humankind.

—Warren Meyer
1956

How to Let God Help You

MY FAITH

I do not believe in evil. I believe in Good.
I do not believe in sin. I believe in Truth.
I do not believe in want. I believe in
    Abundance.
I do not believe in death. I believe in Life.
I do not believe in ignorance. I believe in
    Intelligence.
There are no discords in my being.
    Being is peace.
My faith, understanding, and love
    are becoming one.
"What therefore God hath joined together,
    let not man put asunder."

Dated: 1897

THE PURPOSE OF LIVING

I JUST WANT to come in and have a visit with you. Let us forget all that has pressed itself in upon us, to make us sometimes feel that God the Good is not all in all.

Here, in the silence, we shall know the Presence of God, and see clearly just how we are to go about living the life that He is giving us so we may bring forth the order, beauty, and freedom that He has planned and that are now awaiting our understanding use. But let us not go too far into the metaphysics of this wonderful thing. Instead, we are here together, just to rest quietly and happily in reality. As we do this, a real transformation will be worked in us and for us. We shall reap the good fruits of our study, affirmation, and meditation.

We know from our experience in Unity that there is almost a universal lack of understanding of the Truth of Being. When we use the word *Truth*, we mean that which is true of God, and true of God's children. This spiritual Truth is that you are God's own beloved child and that God is ever giving you His own wisdom, love, power, life, and substance.

In the past we have been led to believe that we are the children of physical parents and that we must get our impressions and education, form our living habits, and even do our work, in the way that they direct. Because of this, we have failed to wake up and find out that we are really God's children and that we have inherited from Him a perfect mind which is capable of unfolding the wonderful Christ qualities, as Jesus Christ unfolded His God-given mind.

As we become aware of the truth that we are God's children and that God is the very intelligence within us, we discover that health also is our inheritance from the Father. We learn, too, that there is divine law in life, with established rules that make for health, happiness, and prosperity if we live by them.

As we learn that we are God's children, living here to find out His plan for us, we become more and more interested in studying spiritual things for ourselves. We are no longer willing to accept the opinions of others, nor to live as they live, especially if their ways bring sickness and sorrow. We begin to feel, rightly, that there must be a way of living that will keep us well and happy.

The real purpose of your life is to express the creation of God—to unfold the many departments of your mind which God has planned for you, and which will enable you to know and to do His will. When you know that there is nothing for you to worry about or to fear, you may then relax and feel happy. When you know that living, as God has planned it, here and now, is beautiful and that you can know just what God's plans are for you, you will be really interested in living, won't you?

Chapter 2

THE
NEW WAY

THE SOUL MUST be awakened, brought to a realization of Truth, and encouraged in the righteous use of all the God-given faculties and powers. The individual must be helped to unify his spirit, soul, and body in harmonious spiritual living here and now.

Heretofore, we may not have seen much in life in this world that was particularly pleasing or worth while. Such a meager outlook results from our trying to see life through a little knothole of personality. We have received the messages that our parents, our teachers, our playmates, our pals, our business associates, our friends, our superior officers, and the world in general have given us through our senses. Thus, we have formed biased opinions of the things within and about us: We have seen what appears, because of limited information, and not what God has created, planned, purposed, and held together through the countless ages.

God—my Father and your Father—has

made me to know that no matter what I have done or what others have done to me, He has implanted within me the pattern of perfection. He has given me the life, power, intelligence, and substance out of which I may recreate my soul qualities and my physical structures, and so come forth a new creature. You, too, by studying and proving this Truth can do the same.

Now, because of God's great understanding love which Jesus Christ has helped us to comprehend and realize, we are beginning to catch glimpses of what the Father is and what He has for us and what we are in Truth. We are beginning to learn that life is our gift from the Father, a gift that is never withdrawn, never lessened, never limited by the Giver. We are beginning to enjoy this gift and to yearn to know how to make right use of it so that we may have the fullness of joy and blessings in it. We are starting to discover that we can actually do the splendid things we were created to do and came into the world to do. This realization should send a glow of warmth and happiness, and a quickening of life all through our being.

Truly, it is of great value for us to set to work to perfect anything and everything that we may find that does not measure up to the best that our new light shows us. We shall discover that it is much more important to change and to do that which is really best for our progress and our health than it is to be smugly consistent or to make the excuse that we have always done thus and so it is too late to change now. The moment we discover anything undesirable in our minds or our lives, we should seek to make the changes necessary to bring about that which is desirable.

Do not be concerned if you do not always get from your study and your prayers the results that your senses take cognizance of. Your spiritual awakening is the important thing. It will increase your consciousness of your unity with God Mind and will give you greater freedom of expression through the various centers of consciousness in your body. Your spiritual study will call these disciples (centers) of yours into finer embodiment so that they will be alert and responsive. It will be up to you to give them the true ideas and set them to work, proving the Truth, each in the thing it is called to do.

LIFE IS A SCHOOL

LIFE IS A SCHOOL. The Great Schoolmaster knows just what problems we need to keep us alert and to bring out the wonderful qualities that the Father has measured out for us to come up to. That is our purpose in life, to succeed in bringing forth God's perfect idea of the perfect man.

In the beginning God created man in His own image and likeness, even as He created the little seed to bring forth of its kind. "As lives the flower in the seed, so lives the Christ in me." The germ of God-likeness slumbers in us, and it should be our true aim in being to make manifest this perfect Self, or Christ of God, in our lives.

All of us sooner or later come to the place in our development where we are no longer satisfied to go on living the old life, without the knowledge of our oneness with God, the Source of our being. Sometimes, when we reach this point in our soul's progress, we do not at first know just what is taking place. We may become restless and dissatisfied. We may go through experiences which we do not understand. We may even be tempted to think that our good has gone from us. But just as surely as there is God the one Presence and one Power, we shall find that all is well, and that we are but going from one room, as it were, into another, larger and lighter room.

As we leave old circumstances, beliefs, habits, and desires behind, and seek to understand and to enter into and get the blessings out of the larger life which is ever opening to us, we are filled with a sense of peace, freedom, and assurance that all is well. We should then turn our attention within and devote ourselves to those thoughts and acts which make for poise, order, health, and success.

As we realize that we are God's children, that we have power and authority to think and to speak the good and true and to have it manifest in harmonious relations and pleasant surroundings, we no longer invite or submit to inharmony, misunderstandings, or limitations. We place ourselves in God's keeping and think Truth, and it directs us in ways of peace and pleasantness.

As we think of others as God's children, we see them in a new light. We understand how it is that they are trying to unfold and use the faculties and powers God has implanted in them, and we have compassion if they seem to fall short at times. We also have power to speak Truth for them, to bless them, and to help them.

"Blessed are they that hunger and thirst after righteousness: for they shall be filled" (Mt. 5:6). All of us are hungering and thirsting after righteousness. All of us are learning how to receive that which feeds and satisfies us. So, you may rejoice this moment that the Holy Spirit is blessing you with the very things you need, and will continue to show you more and more of Truth, until you put on the full Christ consciousness.

Do not bother about anything that has been, or that seems to be taking place at present, or that is to come in the future. Leave past, present, and future in God's hands. Leave yourself in God's care and keeping, and just do that which will furnish Spirit with the necessary co-operation and the necessary materials to be converted into harmony of soul, strength, and health of body. Keep your thoughts free from worry. Keep them on matters close at hand, on God's presence and power.

Sometimes the soul gets so anxious about what it wishes to do that it tends to neglect the body. This is not fair to the body, nor to those who must take care of the body when it is neglected. Your first duty, then, is to bless your body. Get your thoughts right down into it, and praise its wonderful work. Learn what it needs and arrange for supplying those needs.

Sometimes things happen, in the realm of the senses, or in connection with the physical body, which cause one to depreciate the body, or even to wish, almost, that one did not have it. In such an event, the soul may reach out so much that the body is neglected until it suffers. Suffering is one of the means of drawing the attention of the soul back to its beautiful temple. The Christ Mind can and will direct the soul in taking up its wonderful work in the body, that it may continue to have this very necessary vehicle of expression. The light of the Christ Mind enables one to see all things in right relation, so that peace can prevail.

We believe that the whole creation responds to man's consciousness. If at times some of the lesser creations or formations disturb him or his possessions, he should study to change his way, or learn more about the part of the race mind that has caused the malformation. Learning to understand the divine plan of life, and being obedient to it, gives wisdom in dealing with the undesirable tendencies. We should declare that there is one Intelligence, one Power, one Life, and one Substance, and that no destructive elements will counteract these righteous expressions of God Ideas. God will establish order within and without. God's law of equalization is effective everywhere. For everything that has its place upon the earth, there is righteous satisfaction, and there is plenty for all under divine law.

We should help others to get away from the old race beliefs about life: that we are born, grow to maturity, have children, rear them, and then decline and die. We can and must help others to catch the higher vision of living, the development of soul qualities that make life a beautiful and helpful experience. There is so much to be seen and learned and done, that surely one cannot experience all of it in "threescore and ten years."

I am convinced that we are coming to the time when we shall be obliged to face eternal life—to bring the soul face to face with the Christ power, and to hold it to the true course of life until the real plan of life is known and fulfilled. The eating of the tree of the knowledge of good and evil resulted in man's finding what he thought was a way out of his shortcomings: giving up and going to sleep. Most of us have outgrown that childish way. We have taken it upon ourselves to learn about the uses of the mind, so that we are waking up our faculties and discovering the law of health. Now we must learn what is truly worth while and devote ourselves to it. As we do this, we shall find that we are independent; that we really can decide for ourselves what we will do, and carry out the plans.

You are a three-fold being. No doubt you have learned from your Bible that the Spirit of God dwells in man and gives him breath, and that man has a soul and a physical body. But have you really studied these facts, tried to understand them, that you may know how to use this threefold character in the way that God intends?

We have learned that the very presence, life, and intelligence of God are ever abiding in man's being. The Spirit of God is what gives you intelligence and life. Spirit has developed for you the mental life which we call the soul. The soul has built the body and ever continues to renew and rebuild it day by day.

Spirit has no age; it is eternal, as God is eternal and unchanging. The soul is not old in the sense of being full of years and decrepitude. The soul is ever unfolding God's ideas, and these are unchangeable. The development of soul qualities causes the individual to be more and more mature in his judgments and his expressions. The soul ever keeps in touch with that which is true of God and the Son of God, and is ever refreshed and eager for life's experiences.

The body, which is formed by the action of thoughts of life, love, substance, power, and intelligence in everyone, is never old. The very substance out of which the body is formed, and which nourishes and sustains it, is ever new and responsive to the thoughts of life which impress it.

We know that the body is periodically renewed. We can renew and rebuild it and change its appearance by changing our thoughts and living habits.

First of all, remember that God is omnipresent—as present as the very life in which you live, move, and have your being; the very substance out of which your body is formed and nourished; the very intelligence which is within you, in every nerve, brain cell, and structure of the body. God is the very love which draws together and holds in perfect harmony (if you will only allow it) all the elements of your being. God is the very Light which enables you to understand yourself, others, and all God's creation, so that you may always think Truth, the true state of all creation.

Pray for understanding. Claim your oneness with God. Study your relationship with Him so that you may know how to lay hold of the abundant life, intelligence, substance, and love, so that you can build these into your soul and your body, to perfect your expression.

When you have come to the place where you are ready to co-operate with the Source of all good—your indwelling Lord—you are bound to receive His help.

From the beginning, all of the qualities and capabilities you need in order to make for yourself a perfect destiny have been implanted in you. Through your study, understanding, and practice of Truth principles you are finding how to awaken, develop, and set free into righteous expression all of these inner spiritual resources.

Set aside regular periods every day for prayer—times that are most convenient for you. Use words of Truth during your silence periods. As you change your thinking and bring it into line with Truth principles, a transformation will take place in your consciousness. Your mind will become keen, awake, alert, illumined, and your body temple will be filled with new life. You will be inspired with new and practical ideas that will enable you to succeed in a larger way.

SPIRITUAL SCIENCE

Chapter 4

WE ARE STUDYING spiritual science to get a broader conception of God, rather than holding to the view that He is a personal being with parts like man, a being subject to change and capable of varying moods. Though personal to each one of us, God is *IT*, neither male nor female, but *Principle*. God is not a cold, senseless principle like that of mathematics, but the Principle of life, love, and intelligence.

God is All-Intelligence; there is but the one Mind and in reality there are no separate men and women. A full realization of this great Truth would do away with all selfishness, the cause of all the misery of earth. We must understand clearly that the real life of all men is identical with our own and that aside from the one life all is illusion; that all seeming differences in people are caused by selfishness or desire for something separate and apart from God, or our fellow men. Hence, all undue accumulations of money or power by individuals are in direct violation of the divine law. Just to the extent that man tries to claim anything as his personal property, so does he wander away from God the Principle of goodness, equity, love, truth, justice, health, and harmony.

The momentous question is, "How can man come into harmony with Principle?" The answer is, "By simply recognizing that in his real, inner Self man is the expression of Principle, and that seeming sin, sickness, and death are not real." To some this recognition comes easily while to others it is a matter of growth; but it will come to all who persistently seek. We must learn to declare our *oneness* with Principle, regardless of appearances. "Judge righteous judgment" (Jn. 7:24). Along with our declarations of oneness with Principle, we should keep ourselves purified and deny the errors with which false belief has clothed the phenomenal world. As we do "the works" spiritually the results will surely follow.

We are studying a spiritual science as exact in its requirements, as logical in its deductions, and as demonstrable in its workings as the science of mathematics. Exactness and pure reason are the absolute requirements of every successful student. As the fundamental rules of addition, subtraction, multiplication, and division enter into and work out the abstruse problem of the advanced mathematician or the simple example of the beginner, so do the fundamental principles of spiritual science work unerringly in simple healing or in the solution of the great problems of life.

There is mathematical rigor in the demand of this science for absolute correctness of demonstration before the student is able to proclaim his answer correct. We never hear of the "absurdity" of mathematics because it deals with things beyond the sense. On the contrary, everybody trusts this mighty arm that reaches up and counts the stars and measures the shining universe. Everybody believes in the mathematician's unfailing power to compute the day and moment of the reappearance of a comet or the darkening of the sun or moon by eclipse. Of course, it seems very wonderful to those who are familiar with only its fundamental principles to see mathematics reach up and out and solve the secrets of all dimension. Yet, they believe because it is demonstrated—and that is wise.

Now, dear student, the three essentials to success in the study of mathematics are also the three essentials to success in the study of spiritual science. They are: understanding of its fundamental principles; pure and unbiased reasoning; ability to prove that the principle is workable.

The great problem we shall work up to admits of no guesswork. It has been bungled too long; we can no longer hope for a solution from the old statements concerning the problems of life. Everyone who is toiling over this knotty problem knows that its answer is *satisfaction*. The living demonstration of this answer is: knowledge of Truth, peace of mind, health of body. Religion and science have both made statements that their adherents claimed would give the right answer to the problem, but they demonstrated sickness, death, restlessness, dread of evil, useless faith, and profitless knowledge. Certainly these are not the proofs of *satisfaction*. The scientists and the religionists have formed some very absurd equations from their illogical reasonings.

The religionist starts out with the great axiom: "God is All—all Good, all Power, all Wisdom, all Presence." Then, when he takes up the problems of life, he introduces false quantities and establishes false theorems, for he says: "There is a quantity in life called *evil* which equals good in power." Now, don't you see what a mess he makes of it when he goes to form an equation? He started out with the axiom that God is all and God is good. Good plus evil is both a logical and mathematical absurdity. Where good is, evil (its opposite) cannot exist. Pure reasoning from the axiom, "God, the causing power, is all," reduces evil to zero and the problems of life are resolved to the simple equation: "All Good equals satisfaction."

Studying cause and principle throughout the world's history, we find records of the wise children of men who have turned from the absurdity of effect trying to deal with itself, and sought for the great Cause of all. In the study of it they have found that the Causing Power is Mind, and only through knowledge of this Power shall man be able to deal successfully with those restless shadows called human life that appear upon the external canvas of eternity. Those who have had such knowledge have produced at will all the phenomena of effect, and have been called "miracle workers" and "inspired of God." They have been worshiped sometimes as saints and gods; but more often this inconsistent world has turned upon them and trampled them, driving them into hiding or compelling them to take themselves from this canvas of human existence.

It has proved a dangerous experiment in some stages of the world's history to know and speak the truth of this *seeming* called life. But two thousand years ago there came a manifestation of human life so conversant with the great Causing Power of life that He called that power "Father" and it was said of Him, "the Word became flesh" (Jn. 1:14). He was a fearless teacher of Truth. He spent his ministry freeing mankind from delusions. With the sweeping proclamation, "Call no man your father on the earth: for one is your Father, even he who is in heaven" (Mt. 23:9), he emancipated the race from the limitation of mortal parentage.

He taught continually, "Judge not according to appearance" (Jn. 7:24). He denied the right of sensuous taste to command Him, and said, "Man shall not live by bread alone, but by every word that proceedeth out of the mouth of God" (Mt. 4:4). He denied the right of carnal ambition to demand a display of His Power, and said, "Thou shalt not tempt the Lord thy God" (Mt. 4:7 KJV). He denied that (mortal) self was privileged to urge upon Him the kingdom and glories of the earth that were His through divine understanding. He said: "Get thee hence, Satan: for it is written, Thou shalt worship the Lord thy God, and him only shalt thou serve" (Mt. 4:10). It was He who said, "I have overcome the world" (Jn. 16:33). It was He who demonstrated that the problems of life are within every man's power to solve. The false quantities were presented to him with all the sophistries of self just as they were presented to primitive man, and as they are presented to us. But with the clear, broad denial, "Get thee hence," he erased the false statement (evil) man had so long puzzled over, and wrote clear and bold across the board of eternity, *Thou shalt serve good alone.* Good equals satisfaction; satisfaction equals life.

Chapter 5

A SAVING SCIENCE

WE ARE INDEBTED to Jesus Christ and His fearless propagation of Truth for our knowledge of this saving science. He demonstrated that sin, sickness, and death are false quantities and are no part of a correct statement of life. He declared, "If a man keep my word, he shall never see death" (Jn. 8:51). Those who believed in false quantities rose up and confronted Him with the proof of their reasoning. They said: "Abraham died, and the prophets; and thou sayest, If a man keep my word, he shall never taste of death....Whom makest thou thyself?" (Jn. 8:52-53) (The world today is taking the same stand against those who declare that Jesus Christ's words will demonstrate.) But He, straight and true to the axiom, "God is good, and God is all," answered their false logic: "It is my Father that glorifieth me; of whom ye say, that he is your God; and ye have not known him: but I know him; and if I should say, I know him not, I shall be like unto you, a liar: but I know him, and keep his word.... Before Abraham was born, I am" (Jn. 8:54-55, 58).

Again He said: "I know that his commandment is life eternal; the things therefore which I speak, even as the Father hath said unto me, so I speak.... If ye keep my commandments, ye shall abide in my love; even as I have kept my Father's commandments, and abide in his love" (Jn. 12:50, 15:10). Jesus demonstrated that the keeping of His Father's commandments saved from sin, sickness, sorrow, and death. He demonstrated that by His keeping His Father's sayings all power was given to Him "in heaven and on earth": power to control the elements, power to turn water into wine, power to increase loaves and fishes, power to make Himself visible or invisible at will, power to command the fish of the sea to yield Him money, power to lay down His life and power to take it up. Of this wonderful power He said, "I speak not from myself: but the Father abiding in me doeth his works" (Jn. 14:10). He declared of those who believed on Him as He believed on the Father, "The works that I do shall he do also; and greater works than these shall he do; because I go unto the Father" (Jn. 14:12). Jesus Christ taught distinctly that "one is your Father, even he who is in heaven," and that "the kingdom of God is within you."

Who can mistake the Truth? Our Father

has His kingdom in man and of a truth makes good the promise, "According to your faith be it done unto you" (Mt. 9:29). Jesus puts it, "Believe me that I am in the Father, and the Father in me: or else believe me for the very works' sake" (Jn. 14:11).

Jesus Christ made of every statement a living thing. What has been called His teaching is not His teaching if it will not heal the sick and feed the poor, as He said it would. It has been this fact that has caused so much unbelief in the teachings of this age. The mistake some of our teachers make is that they believe in Christ intellectually and deal with His truths intellectually—whereas spiritual things must be "spiritually judged." They have no conception of the esoteric meaning of Jesus Christ's words and consequently have no power to demonstrate them. It is the spiritually blind leading the blind, and they have fallen "into a pit" of mortal error. We find preachers of the ways of life diseased and feeble, devout and pious Christians fearful and unhappy, the gentle and kindhearted suffering from extreme poverty. Not of such did Jesus say, "I am glorified in them" (Jn. 17:10). It is of such unfruitful teachers that He said: "Ye took away the key of knowledge: ye entered not in yourselves, and them that were entering in ye hindered" (Lk. 11:52).

There are many now who "turn" the key of knowledge and enter into the understanding of what Jesus Christ meant when He declared, "He that believeth on me, the works that I do shall he do also." They prove their understanding by doing the very works He did. One gentle-hearted little woman lately was the channel for healing a baby of as severe a type of leprosy as any recorded among the healings of Jesus. Another teacher of spiritual science was instrumental in causing a cataract to melt from a man's eye by one treatment. The film gradually slipped off. I have seen the lame rise up and walk, and fever depart as recorded in the word of the Gospel.

These are the "signs" to follow. They indicate the *true* believer. The truths which were spoken in secret (in esoteric language) shall be "proclaimed upon the housetops" of high understanding. After this great spiritual wave sweeps over the earth, every remaining inhabitant shall know Him, "whom to know aright is life eternal," and whom to serve aright is joy everlasting.

FUNDAMENTAL PROPOSITIONS

Chapter

6

Jesus taught certain great propositions as the law of God. He spent much time communing with God and knew more of God than any other who ever lived. To find out what He taught is to find true life. He declared, "I am the way, and the truth, and the life: no one cometh unto the Father, but by me.... The word which ye hear is not mine, but the Father's who sent me" (Jn. 14:6, 24). This substantiates John's description of Jesus, "the Word became flesh." Jesus declared that the Scriptures were full of the same teachings He was giving, and that Moses had rightly called God the creator of all. Moses taught the whole story of God, man, and life in the first chapter of Genesis. He taught, "In the beginning God created." This is also rendered, "In the great forever, without beginning of years or end of days, God is revealing or creating." In other words, God is responsible for all that is *real.*

Jesus said, "God is spirit" (Jn. 4:24 RSV).

29

Spirit, then, is responsible for all that is *real*. "God is love" (1 Jn. 4:8). Love, then, is Creator of all that is *real*. That which is not of love and by love is not real. God is Truth. So, Truth is Creator of all that is *real*, and that which is not of Truth and by Truth is not real. God is life. Therefore life is the great Creator and Cause of all that is *real*, and that which is not of life and by life is not real. God is the only substance. So, God being Spirit, Spirit is the only substance.

Now, that which is All must be *omnipresent*. That which is All can have no opposing power, so it must be *omnipotent*. That which is All must contain all wisdom, hence it must be *omniscient*. *Allness* sweeps the great circle of eternity clear of everything but Itself. What else can lay claim to any points within this great creative All? We have a law in physics which says, "Two bodies cannot occupy the same space at the same time." You smile at the very absurdity of denying it. Yet, remember, there are those who, calling themselves scientific, yet declare that though "God is all and God is love," there is still room for a devil; that though "God is all and God is life," there is still room for sickness and death. However these persons manage to explain such inconsistencies to their own satisfaction matters not to us, for we know that they have departed from law and reason and that the shadows they are calling realities cannot stand as *substance* before the dawning of the great sun of pure reasoning.

Spiritual science, after starting out with the generally accepted basic principle, "God is All," keeps straight on in pure and unadulterated logic. It puts fairly to everyone questions which from their own premises will each admit but one answer. Spiritual science says: "If God is all and God means *Good,* Genesis must read, 'In the beginning *Good* created.' Can Good create evil? If God is Love, then 'In the beginning *Love* created.' Can Love create hatred and torment? If God is Truth, 'In the beginning *Truth* created.' Can Truth create error? If God is Life, then, 'In the beginning *Life* created.' Can Life create death?"

If you have answered these questions in pure reason, you must admit that Genesis records no *false* creations. Now, put in order the glorious sequence you have never correctly arranged before. Call this great creative principle by any of its wonderful names: God, Life, Love, Mind, Spirit. It is ever present, all-powerful, all-wise, eternal. In it "we live, and move, and have our being" (Acts 17:28). It is the loving, wise, power-bestowing Father of whom Jesus said, "All things whatsoever the Father hath are mine" (Jn. 16:15). It is the God "whom to know aright is life eternal." It is the great Parent who has begotten us: "One is your Father, even he who is in heaven." God, the great Mind, conceived us, generated us out of Himself. We are His. His perfect expression is coming forth into manifestation. This manifestation is the state called right-eousness (right thinking). The Psalmist says in Psalms 17:15:

> "I shall behold thy face
> in righteousness;
> I shall be satisfied, when I awake,
> with beholding thy form."

Now, you have taken steps in right think-ing. You have reasoned out the *true* of life. If you will obey Jesus' direction, you will attain righteousness. He says, "Judge not according to appearance, but judge righteous judg-ment." This means: Shut out of your mind that which *looks* real and hold firmly to the thought of what *is* real. Stop thinking that evil is real. Think of good as all. Stop thinking that matter is real. Know that Spirit is all.

To do this is to lift yourself into health and peace. "He that ... shutteth his eyes from looking upon evil: he shall dwell on high" (Is. 33:15-16). "Except one be born of water and the Spirit [Mind], he cannot enter into the kingdom of God" (Jn. 3:5). "Flesh and blood cannot inherit the kingdom of God" (1 Cor. 15:50). "The kingdom of God cometh not with observation: neither shall they say, Lo, here! or, There! for lo, the kingdom of God is within you" (Lk. 17:20-21). Jesus Christ's whole teaching bore upon the necessity of every man's getting out of the sensual mind and entering into the kingdom of his Father (pure Mind). "It is the spirit that giveth life; the flesh profiteth nothing: the words that I have spoken unto you are spirit, and are life.... He that is of God heareth the words of God" (Jn. 6:63, 8:47).

Jesus said to those who professed righteousness yet lived in the sensuous mind, and judged according to appearances: "Ye are of your father the devil, and the lusts of your father it is your will to do. He was a murderer from the beginning, and standeth not in the truth, because there is no truth in him. When he speaketh a lie, he speaketh of his own: for he is a liar, and the father thereof" (Jn. 8:44). Was there ever a broader, clearer denial of the unreality of all outside the great Mind of Truth? If a lie were *true* or *real*, it would not be a lie, would it?

A thing to be *true* or *real* must have Truth in it, then, must it not? If then, as Jesus distinctly states of the one whom He called the devil, "there is no truth in him," how do you make him a reality? If his claims are all lies, and he is the father of lies, how can you conceive of sensuous man as a reality? If he is a murderer from the beginning, he is father of death. Does that prove that death is real? Can falsehood be the father of Truth? Jesus said: "If a man keep my word, he shall never

33

see death." "I am the way, and the truth, and the life: no one cometh unto the Father, but by me." "If ye abide in my word, then are ye truly my disciples; and ye shall know the truth, and the truth shall make you free" (Jn. 8:31-32). Christ means Truth.

Now, through keen reasoning, we arrive at the *real* concerning life. Here we have Jesus Christ as authority to bear us out in our conclusions. He declares that the devil is a lie, which means an unreality. Sensuous man is the child of a lie (the creation of unreality). Everything spoken of this unreality or by this unreality *is* unreal. Now we are ready to turn our back on this lie and enter into the kingdom of the Father whose "righteousness is an everlasting righteousness" (Ps. 119:142).

Put off, then, the lying tongue. Take up the words of Spirit, and of Life. Put off the habit of thinking lying thoughts; think of life, truth, and love as the only reality. Put off the habit of listening to unprofitable conversation. God within has the voice to which you should listen, the voice that will lead you into all Truth.

But remember that you cannot enter the kingdom of mind weighed down and piled high with old burdens of false notions and prejudices. As has been said, "It is easier for a camel to go through a needle's eye, than for" such a man "to enter into the kingdom of God" (Mt. 19:24). It is only the pure in mind

34

who see God. They who keep the oil of Truth burning in their lamps of understanding can enter into and partake of this marriage feast. They who would behold God's face in righteousness must awake in this likeness of mind. We train the mind to such likeness by right words. We train the mind to righteousness by beginning back at its very Source and stopping every thought but the right one. There is no right foundation thought but the true thought of Creator, creation, and existence. God is Creator. We are creation. We exist or show forth our Creator. We are not showing forth, therefore, except as we show forth *good*. We show forth good by our word. "The words that I have spoken unto you are spirit, and are life." "The Word was God ... and without him was not anything made that hath been made" (Jn. 1:1-3). The Word is God. We show forth God by acknowledging Spirit only. Stop every thought but the thought that *Spirit is All.* God is Spirit. God makes all. Spirit is the substance out of which all things are made.

As already stated, before we can enter into the kingdom of God (Spirit or Mind) which opens to us through this new way of thinking and living, we must drop old prejudices and old thoughts and sit meekly down to learn what is true. We must let go of old beliefs in sin, sickness, and death. We need not worry about what will become of them any more than we need give thought to the place where darkness flees when the light is brought in, or to where cold goes when the fire is lighted on our hearth, or to what becomes of ignorance when knowledge takes its place. When you realize that Spirit is All, that Truth shall set you free from negative conditions, they all go just where darkness and cold are when driven away by the energies of light and heat: nowhere.

Then shall you awake in the likeness of Spirit and behold in righteousness the face of Truth; then shall the genesis of your new heavenly and earthly satisfaction read: "In the beginning Love, Good, and Life created the thoughts that people my world. Peace flows through it as a river; glory and gladness roof its skies; joy and health are the morning and evening stars; willing service is the moon that follows after the great sun of righteousness; understanding is the soil where springs forth the beauty of action. The angel that guards the Eden of my world is purity of thought. My love of life is absolute knowledge of Truth." This is your world, created by the mind that was in Christ Jesus.

DENIAL AND AFFIRMATION

"Back of the canvas that throbs, the painter
  is hinted and hidden;
Into the statue that breathes, the soul of the
  sculptor is bidden;
Under the joy that is felt, lies the infinite
  issue of feeling;
Crowning the glory revealed is the glory that
  crowns the revealing.
Great are the symbols of Being but that
  which is symboled is greater;
Vast the created and beheld, but vaster the
  inward Creator."

JESUS TAUGHT in the shining of a perfect life.
He said: "I sanctify myself, that they themselves also may be sanctified in truth.... And
the glory which thou hast given me I have
given unto them" (Jn. 17:19, 22). He had first
taught them, however, that sanctification
came by denial.

Jesus Christ's denials in the wilderness
sent from Him the lingering darkness of mor-

37

tal sense and revealed to Him the glory of His Father's full light. He commanded, "Call no man your father on the earth," and affirmed, "for one is your Father, even he who is in heaven." Being obedient to His righteous judgment, we accept the name Christ for the crowning of our spiritual science, and put behind us, as He did, the claims of earthly parentage. We boldly deny evil. We deny sin, sickness, and death. Jesus denied death by glorious resurrection.

These things are not put away by denials. They are only there as a false sense. Denials put away the false sense and we see as we are seen by the great spiritual Father of all.

Denial seems to be the rock of offense in our Zion. Good people of the old mind say: "The teachings of spiritual science are beautiful—the results of your demonstrations are satisfactory—but why must you spoil it all by those odious denials? Why, you make yourselves professional liars!"

To one such person we recommended that he stretch his tender conscience enough to try denial on the rheumatism that plagued him. He reported that the pain left him but he prayed God to forgive the lie. "If any man would come after me, let him deny himself, and take up his cross, and follow me" (Mt. 16:24). "This is the judgment," said Jesus, "that the light is come into the world, and men loved the darkness rather than the light"

(Jn. 3:19).

Paul explains this man's case exactly in the statement, "Now the natural man receiveth not the things of the Spirit of God: for they are foolishness unto him; and he cannot know them, because they are spiritually judged" (1 Cor. 2:14). Plato said, "It is demonstrated to us, that if we are designed to know any thing purely, we must be liberated from the body and behold things with the soul." This was the liberty of Christ. And so successful was the propagation at the time of Paul that he gave "thanks unto the Father ... who delivered us out of the power of darkness, and translated us into the kingdom of the Son of his love" (Col. 1:12-13).

Philosophy teaches that all that was ever known exists in the world of ideas. When we are able to rise into this realm, we shall know all things. But, in order to rise into it, we must learn to forget the false sense of the body. This false sense is the great gulf between us and the kingdom. Thus, the denial erases the false statement we have so long been making and leaves us free to commence anew.

Now, we add the active principle of affirmation, and lo, the solution to our problem will demonstrate. We find we can dissolve the earthly house of false beliefs by denial and enter into the "house not made with hands" by affirmation. Our divine Being steps into its eternal inheritance (wisdom) and by intuition becomes unerringly guided by her shining light to a stage that is well, happy, strong, and noble. When the mind opens by speaking denials, this *true Self* that philosophers have so long striven to free shows itself all glorious with wisdom, strength, and holiness. When we see the glory of the Good, we lay hold upon the Good we see with great words of welcome. We make the welding binding by affirmations.

But our words must be trained, or we do not see the Good. It is written: "Take with you words, and return unto Jehovah" (Hos. 14:2). An angel is a word of Truth. Denial of evil is a word of Truth. Affirmation of Good is a word of Truth. These angels shall constantly have charge over us if we fail them not. They shall bear us up that we dash not our foot against the cruel beliefs of the flesh. But we must be faithful and orderly in speaking these words of Truth or we shall be left in the wilderness of sense. To speak Truth faithfully is a healing stream. Pure reasoning is a healing stream; its strengthening flow makes all crooked places straight.

As the shining forth of the sun brings out the wealth of meadows, the beauty and fragrance of the rose, or the full corn to the husk, so shall the shining divinity of each of us call forth wealth, peace, health, and love where all had seemed a wilderness of sorrow.

Only steady shining Truth can accomplish this. We cannot divide the mind with doubt. We cannot divide the thought with sense. To be double-minded is to be unstable in all our ways. "Unstable as water, thou shalt not excel" (Gen. 49:4 KJV).

Chapter 8

THE EMBODIMENT OF THOUGHT

ANCIENT WISDOM teaches that we are the result of what we have thought—we are made up of our thoughts. Solomon puts it, "As he thinketh within himself, so is he" (Prov. 23:7).

The operations of thought are not understood in detail by the ordinary man and we cannot apply the logical deductions of speculation in a realm where specific forms are built up and vivified with a seeming life through certain modes of thinking. Every thought molds from the etheric essence a form symbol, which symbol has a certain degree of temporary life, and by virtue of that life impresses itself upon the body. Hence thoughts have their hidden law with which those who are experienced have become familiar, and it is safe to follow their directions until you arrive at a stage of unfoldment where you know for yourself.

Now, it is evident that the condition of error in which humanity finds itself at the present period is the result of ages and ages of wrong thinking, and as "thoughts are things," before we can get a flood of new concepts we must clear away the old. It has been found that this can be done most effectively by the disintegrating power of denial. In some instances the great errors of the race have become universal beliefs and have been formulated as laws and are regarded by the mass of the human family as the immortal creations of the Supreme Ruler. It becomes, then, a necessity that we keep with all diligence this inward Creator of our external creation. "Power belongs to him who knows." And when we are thoroughly translated into the knowledge that "the lower world is made after the pattern of the upper and inner world," then will we have power over all these appearances of sense.

This inner world is the subjective, the *real* world, the *intelligible* world. Plato talked much about it as "the home of the soul"; the Christians sighed for "the kingdom of heaven." Having such knowledge, you will realize that Mind is the great white throne of omnipotence. Good sits enthroned there; Love sits enthroned there; Life sits enthroned there. You may approach the throne boldly. You may claim all of these blessings with your divine thought for they are surely yours. There is no uncertainty. "All things whatsoever the Father hath are mine," says Pure Mind. "If ye shall ask anything of the Father,

he will give it you in my name. This is knowing God aright. This is life eternal. This is the
faith of the lilies."

How different from this is that imperfect
faith that keeps its possessor trembling with
terror and apprehension, keeping one eye on
the stock exchange or the pill business. There
is an uncertainty about those who trust only
people or gold.

"Put out into the deep, and let down your
nets for a draught" (Lk. 5:4). Take hold of the
Great Mind with your thoughts. Lay firm hold
of the Good that God has furnished for the
taking. "Perfect love casteth out fear" (1 Jn.
4:18). If we love the Truth we are not afraid.
We are bold to put out into the sea of faith
and let down our healing thoughts. They do
the work and the nets break with the good
things that come to us. We have perfect trust
in almighty Truth.

To the average person faith is rather an
indefinite quality on the ordinary plane of
sense, and few regard it as the most important faculty of mind. Yet we find in the study
of metaphysics that no other faculty is so
often called into play in the demonstration of
spiritual science. Faith ceases to be the
vague, illusive quality which traditional
Christianity theorizes about, and takes on a
strong tangibility. We find that the realm of
mind includes a country much more substantial and real than this of matter. In fact, the

material world is but a fleeting shadow of the unseen. This has been known to the students of Truth in all ages, but it is just now becoming the knowledge of men universally.

On this unseen plane of causes, all things move by laws. But man is so deluded by the five senses and has depended upon them for information so implicitly that he has lost sight of this higher realm of causes. Hence when he is told that a certain line of thought held strongly in the mind will produce certain effects, he will not believe it. Here, then, comes that quality of faith. He must by a mighty effort believe that God is all-powerful and all-good, and that His creation must be likewise. Hence there must somewhere be that which will respond to his righteous appeal. The changes in the mental atmosphere are frequently of a nature to produce the most discouraging conditions, yet he must not waver from his allegiance to principle. No matter what the appearances may be, he must hold strenuously to the only tenable basis: "All is Good," and its manifestations must by the law of logic be likewise. "Delight thyself also in Jehovah; And he will give thee the desires of thy heart" (Ps. 37:4). That is, you are now in a country the laws of which you do not know, and all you can do is trust your unseen guide, secure in the thought that if you are faithful all will be well in the end.

"God is no respecter of persons" (Acts 10:34). The light of heaven shines alike upon the just and the unjust. Truth's ever-shining light is for all alike and sends its messages of divine splendor to all. Keep your soul open to the shining light of Truth by denial of past or future claims upon you, for you live in the *now*. Affirm the *now* as your only active eternity. So shall Truth descend in full power upon you—not divided by past memories or future desires, but bursting with present fulfillment. No mortal lie can creep into the glory of the ever-present *now*. No cloud of doubt can hover over such present certainty.

The trusting student of Truth rests on these words of Daniel: "Thy kingdom shall be sure unto thee, after that thou shalt have known that the heavens do rule" (Dan. 4:26). The student should never comment on error. He should, instead, go back of it all into the inner, clean light of reason and see all persons free from false judgments. He should fully realize that he is his brother's keeper and must guard with sacred care every thought that goes out to his brother, lest like Cain he spill innocent blood. Oh, too sacred is the vitalizing energy of thought to drag it down with the mire of false judgment.

"Keep thy heart with all diligence;
For out of it are the issues of life."
—Proverbs 4:23

If things take on a dark look, cleanse your mind with denials. If a feeling of emptiness comes over you, a feeling of desolation or of ignorance, pull yourself back into the full stature of Truth by repeated affirmations. To deny all the time is unwise. Every denial should be followed by an affirmation.

(Some people are very orderly in their holding of spiritual thoughts. They take Monday for the statement of being. They deny all day Tuesday. They affirm all day Wednesday. They state their absolute faith on Thursday. On Friday they declare every word an effectual, working agent for good. On Saturday they declare themselves perfect in the sight of an understanding God and praise His works. They wait in the silence on Sunday. If they are treating others, they use the same formula. Their plan has been a productive and thorough work.)

"Order is heaven's first law." When the word of God is kept constantly in the heart there is no place for error. Sure healing is attained by him who ever keeps the portal of his thought guarded by these two angels: denial and action. "The words that I have spoken unto you are spirit, and are life," said Jesus—and His words were alive, for His mind was quickened by Spirit.

In metaphysics we learn the immense importance of words. "Every idle word that men shall speak, they shall give account thereof.... For by thy words thou shalt be justified, and by thy words thou shalt be condemned" (Mt. 12:36-37). Let us remember this when tempted to give weight to false judgment. Physics makes actions alone responsible for results, but the clear-sighted Newton said: "Let physics beware of metaphysics." In dealing with the external he had discovered that unseen laws stand back of all movement. He knew that when physics laid claim to *cause*, it assumed false power which sooner or later would be swept aside as chaff by the truth of metaphysics.

Perhaps a specific error is causing trouble for you. If you are resentful, you cannot do a good healing work till that trait is conquered. If you are impatient and irritable, look for the sweet, fresh bloom that a restful attitude alone can bring you. Some people are sorrowful. "God loveth a cheerful giver"—that is, a giver of cheer. Some persons are dishonest. Some are faultfinding. Some believe in a devil. Some indulge in the belief of a wrathful God. Some feel that God is a respecter of persons and has given their friends better opportunities for happiness and success. Some think God is variable, having times and seasons. All these beliefs keep us from doing good work if we keep them in our consciousness. Also, we convey these beliefs to those around us if we do not put them away. If we are willing to do our part, Spirit will cleanse us white as snow.

Wash and be clean!

Chapter 9

THE MIND
RECEIVES

As YOU STUDY, you will learn that your mind receives from two sources: the universal Mind of Being, which has its outlet through your consciousness, and the intellectual activities of the individual minds about you, which have both conscious and subconscious phases of expression.

Now, that which you receive from the Mind of God is always good, always helpful, health-inspiring and peace-inspiring. That which you receive from the reports of your senses, or the minds of others, may be true and helpful or it may be false and harmful.

The study and practice of Truth will help you to discriminate between the false and the true, and to combine rightly the ideas of the Christ Mind within you, that you may express and bring forth whatsoever you will.

The mind sends *its* messages along the nerves; therefore, you can see that the character of your thoughts does affect the nerves. When the thoughts are of worry, fear, anxiety, grief, lack of life, loneliness, lack of supply, or any other negation, the nerves suffer and become depleted or sore. The nerves, being affected by the mind, get into a chronic condition of cross currents from repeated anxious, worried, fearful, sorrowful thoughts; and many forms of nervousness result.

The treatment, then, is to turn one's attention to God, the indwelling Lord, with the happy assurance that all old, disappointing things are dropping away and the healing, peace-giving, joy-filling, prospering ideas of God's love, life, and substance are filling the mind and heart, quickening new energies in the body.

Now that we know a bit of what we are doing, let us decide why we are doing it! You see, it really is important that you understand the reasons why you are praying for these blessings. For usually it is some lack of vision and purpose, or at least a lack of understanding of the way in which to proceed, that is responsible for the appearance of lack. When we know just what we want and why we want it, we usually find the way opening toward it. If there is need for a different attitude, our attentiveness to Spirit and our willingness to do that which is best, and our confidence that we can do it, give us the light. If there is need for more strength, the happy acknowledgment of God as unlimited life and strength, and our eager use of that strength in doing the very things which appeal, will increase the life flow and prompt the organism to demand that which it requires.

When, in the development of the soul, man became self-conscious he began to discriminate between that which brought desirable results and that which resulted in something undesirable. In order to impress his subconsciousness with the fact that he should avoid the undesirables, he began to name them *evil, sin, devil, adversary: that which is opposed to the good.* Of course, these activities of mind were in operation before man had language, and the feelings and habits were interpreted in words as man grew to know how to put his mental operations into words.

The God of the Old Testament was, therefore, an outgrowth of man's expanding concept of power and the good. But, because he was still in the state where he tried to avoid undesirable results by threatening himself, he attributed these same qualities to his God.

In the study of the Bible, we must understand that those who have received glimpses of the Truth of Being sometimes speak of Jehovah God, or Lord God, and sometimes they refer to God, Elohim, or Creator and Source of all that is.

The Lord God, or Jehovah, is the individual consciousness of God, the Christ Mind unfolding the ideas of God-Mind. Because

God has created man in His image and after His likeness—given him the same qualities and ideas that inhere in God-Mind—man can comprehend the Father, the Creator, Elohim. But because it is man's work to unfold all that God has implanted in him, he is growing; and because he is given freedom and the privilege of interpreting the kingdom individually, he sometimes makes unwise experiments. The experiments are unwise in the sense that the results are not what he desires to continue, but profitable because they give him the lessons of experience. So man's own experiences and growth determine his concept of Jehovah, or the Lord.

Until he awakens in the son-of-God consciousness, and knows that there is but one Presence and Power, the Good Omnipotent, he tells himself, or accepts from the race mind, that there is an adversary or a devil, with which he must deal. When his faculties have developed to the point where he can comprehend spiritual qualities and law, he will not listen to unwise suggestions nor make foolish use of his God-given faculties and powers.

Our salvation is in our living by the Christ pattern—not only by the teachings of the man Jesus Christ but by the Christ Mind within us. Jesus Christ is merging His consciousness with the universal race consciousness, that we may have His presence and the light, power, life, and love which are expressing as our pattern and constant, quickening help.

If you have lived in what men call hell, what of that? Interpreters and translators of the Bible sometimes used the word *hell* to describe refuse grounds. Some of the writers of the Scriptures were trying to show their students how it is that the Holy Spirit of God, active in the lives of men, will put them through a process similar to the purifying fires which were built in a ravine outside cities, where garbage and trash were dumped and burned as a measure of sanitation. These fires were kept burning all the time; and of course, to the things thrown in them, they were destructive. But there is nothing in all the Scripture to cause us to believe that they were in any measure destructive or harmful to man.

Other words that have been interpreted as *hell* referred to graves and pits. Many of the old writers believed that when sinners died and were buried, that was the end of them. But there is no indication here that there was great suffering or torment in the grave or pit. It was simply an end to a thing which error had caused.

We have come to think of hell as a sort of reaping of what has been sown—not a punishment, but rather, a cleansing and purifying process which results in the individual's being brought to face his mistakes and being set free from them and their effects. The work of the Spirit is thorough, and lasts until we measure up to the Jesus Christ standard of life. So long as there is that in us which needs the refining fire of Spirit, we may be sure we can receive its benefits.

Sometimes we seem to have more unpleasant experiences than at other times. If we study the matter, we shall find that we have these unpleasant experiences when we have been tampering with the law. We have taken it upon ourselves to hurry up the growth of another, or of ourselves; we have seen fit— mentally or otherwise—to call attention to shortcomings, and sometimes to condemn another or ourselves. When we do this, we simply stir up and bring forth more of the errors that are in the subconsciousness, and must meet the consequences.

Our teaching is that Jesus Christ is ever with us, and is able to handle all these over- comings in the right way. When we identify ourselves with Him and seek to think, speak, and live in harmony with the ways of Jesus, we get along nicely, and are able to handle each and every situation in a splendid way.

If it seems you are in hell at times, just close your mouth, smile, hold steady, and give thanks that God is there, Jesus Christ is with you, raising you up out of the false beliefs and the effects of shortcomings, and helping you to abide in the pure and free

Mind which expresses in you as joy and sweetness and ability to bless and free others.

Do not brood on things which stir up strife. If it seems that you are in hell, just know that there is a stairway leading from hell to heaven. When there is nothing in you to require the purifying fires, you will rise on the very spiritual atmosphere you have created, into a beautiful new realm of life.

Chapter 10

THE POWER
OF THE WORD

THE VISIBLE UNIVERSE is but the externalization of thoughts. Man, a spiritual word or thought, has existed from the beginning. Hence in reality man's higher Self is spiritual. He is Life and Intelligence expressed. He thinks and his thoughts become objective as forms. These forms are of many grades of density, or as the physical scientist would say, molecular vibration. The *real* man is not of any of these forms; he is the force that causes the forms to exist, and when he knows this, every phase of phenomenal life comes under his dominion. Thus spiritual science teaches that only limited results can be obtained by studying the body or any of its conditions. The body has its origin in the mind and can be successfully regulated only from that point.

The Bible dwells upon the power of the Word, from Genesis to Revelation, and it is surprising that the traditional church has not discovered that "death and life are in the power of the tongue" (Prov. 18:21). John says what all mystics have said, that only the Word existed in the beginning and by it were all things created. The Greek Word *Logos* used by John, which is generally translated *word*, has a double meaning. It means not only the expression of the divine Word, but the *word* based on pure reason or logic. *Logos* is in fact the root of our word *logic*. Thus, we are to understand not only that God created by the power of the Word, but that Word also included logical consistency. That is, God being Spirit, as a logical sequence His creations must be spiritual. We thus arrive at a concise and rational conclusion that all of man that is permanent must of necessity be spiritual. Knowing this to be true and also that the only permanent creation must in some way express the words of Truth, man has but to think right thoughts in order to come into harmonious surroundings.

Nearly every day something that appears new (but which in reality is old) is brought before us. There are in our world today many things of which we knew nothing a few years ago. These things are not new; they have merely come into expression. The world and all that the world contains were created in the beginning. At one time we had nothing to do with the control of electricity, but now we make it one of our servants. It has been given us for our use; we can direct it, and yet we do not know what it is. What we think we know involves so much we do not know that we can hardly say that we really know anything. Yet those who believe in God know that everything is possible with Him. When we come to believe this, we are not astonished at anything. We begin to live; our minds are opened more and more, and we expect wonderful new things to come to us day by day.

In everything we have to consider time, but the time necessary for doing a thing is shortened through understanding. In the old way of studying, it took years to learn arithmetic; now we find that there are short cuts to learning arithmetic. We are beginning to wonder where this elimination of time will stop. We are almost taken off our feet with the new ideas of what we are, for we are learning that we are not what we seem to be. We are not solid flesh and blood; we are really mind and spirit. The more quickly we find this out, the more quickly we apply it in our lives; so our world changes.

What we call disease is lack of harmony in the organism. When we touch the Christ state of consciousness, harmony pours over us, and that which is called illness—a condition resulting from inharmony within ourselves— is corrected by an adjustment of mind. When we become acquainted with one another and know what we are in Truth, we change our minds about one another. The emotions that are called passion and temper are changed; they are spiritualized. Understood, they become powers, wonderful powers.

One can love and yet become angry. Anger has been misunderstood, and, being out of harmony with life, it becomes destructive. When once the emotion behind anger is understood, it can be transformed and made an ally of good. The longing that we call appetite is really aspiration. As long as we think we can satisfy it with something that we can eat or drink, it grows; therefore we have to learn to satisfy the longing with a true consciousness of what it is. It is a thirst after righteousness, which understanding satisfies.

We are learning about the things that were mysterious. We are knowing ourselves better and better; we are finding that there is something in us that understands better than the intellectual self. We are beginning to find a new heaven and a new earth. The things that we have thought to be beyond our ken are gradually coming into our knowledge. We are gradually coming to know that we are one with Him who knows all, one with the one perfect life. We are finding that the Spirit within us is greater than all else.

Since two or more gathered together have the tremendous power that Jesus promised, what power would be released if thousands could be united in speaking one thought! It was this idea which led us to publish monthly thoughts in our Unity periodicals, that we all might unite our thoughts at some time in the day. When we come together in the Spirit, we all are one in the true place of the Most High. Our words become charged with great healing power. As they go forth they can do mighty works.

When we pray together in omnipresence, we lose sight of everything but the one Presence; we recognize only the spiritual Source of all things. In the full understanding and use of this Source is all that our souls have longed for.

As we learn to use the power of the word we discover that we no longer have to beg for that which we think we need and that which satisfies our longings. We find that when we have put away all that hinders us, we are led into our good; it is ours; God gives it to us. He is pouring Himself out upon us as the fullness of all things. We receive not by begging and crying, but by acknowledging and realizing, as Jesus Christ did, our oneness with the Father.

When we have found the kingdom of God and the richness of it, we come into touch with the allness of the one Ruler whose throne is within. Then we have no more trouble about things. Things come just as naturally as the planted seed grows.

Chapter

11

MEETING THE CLOVEN HOOF

WHEN HE OF THE cloven hoof appears "count it all joy," for these times of deviating from the right are the result of the Spirit of Good doing a much needed housecleaning work. Once you become master of yourself, you will not stir up a dust cloud of negativeness when you discover some hidden corner in your mind that needs to be free. In the old days you had to use the broom; now you may use a vacuum cleaner and avoid stirring up large quantities of dust. So you are learning how to use your mental vacuum cleaner in your overcoming and making things easier and more pleasant for those about you.

The unpleasant condition is just temporary, and it is dissolved by the Truth that you are and have been thinking. Just as the best housekeepers use modern appliances to enable them to do their work with the least inconvenience and best results, you are helped by using the spiritual methods in renewing your consciousness and setting your body temple in order. Don't be disturbed by the temporary disorder. See it as the efforts of soul and body to make adjustments, bringing to the surface the things that need attention and the baptism of Spirit.

Suppose a person who had a house furnished with old, uncomfortable furniture were to receive new furniture of great value and practicality. Immediately he would set about the work of cleaning house and preparing the way for the new good. He would put out the old furnishing and make room for the new. During this process his home would not be in the "apple-pie" order it would otherwise manifest. Now, you have received some new and priceless ideas of Christ, the Truth, which are renewing your mind and body. The Christ ideas are becoming organic; that is, they are causing the pure life and substance of Spirit to manifest in every nerve, cell, and fiber of your body temple. Your mind and your body are being transformed and spiritualized because you are getting new "furnishings."

One of the most necessary and important things is that each individual soul be about the things it is embodied to do. When you are doing the will of your own Lord, you are growing, and your soul is radiant and satisfied. You are not repressing your true Self or sitting negative and hungry while others plan for you and dictate what you shall or shall not do. To allow others to control you, openly or according to conventionalities, is to fail to fulfill God's plan in you—and of course you cannot then be happy or healthy. Happiness comes with the realization that you are expressing what God has implanted in you and that you are not in bondage to anyone. To busy yourself with outside affairs, simply to get away from the burdensome thoughts and feelings that arise from the sense of bondage, will not get you anywhere. Such efforts are makeshifts. Make up your mind and heart to put your spirit and soul into *inside* interests, and get real satisfaction out of life. The state we call heaven is awaiting those who are ready for it: the peace and harmony and order that come from living in tune with infinite good.

We understand hell to be a purifying process, which the soul goes through to rid it of dross and weakness. The word *hell* is derived from a word which was used to denote a city incinerator in a valley outside of Jerusalem. Use of the incinerator was a health measure, a means of taking care of the trash of the city. We feel that the Scripture writers were trying to make clear to us the way in which the purifying fire of Spirit continues its work in us until we come forth free from all that does not measure up to the Christ standard. It is for our good, and does not harm us, except we resist it or do not make the effort to give up and to avoid that which caused the undesirable condition of soul, body, or affairs. So, just look yourself over and see what it is that makes it necessary for you to go through "hell" so often, and why each trip seems worse than the last!

Perhaps you have just failed to realize that you are entirely purified and free and ready to enter into the kingdom of peace, order, love, and beauty where the fiery furnaces are not necessary. When there is nothing in your subconsciousness which falls short of the Truth, the Christ standard, you will not feel uncomfortable or find yourself meeting problems that seem without solution. "Purgatory" is but a condition of the soul. It is that which cleanses one of undesirable beliefs and habits. That which is termed purgatory is for your good, and takes away something which has been hindering your progress.

You can bring these undesirable states to an end right now! First of all, stop believing in them, and the necessity for them. Second, make up your mind that you are not going to stand for them, not a moment longer! Third, watch your thoughts and attitudes and acts, to see that you do not invite undesirable states. (Oh, you do not invite them intentionally, of course, but you do invite them in some way, else they could not come to you.)

Some new attitudes will be necessary. Some old customs and beliefs will have to be

65

changed and given up. A new side of you will have to be shown. A new disregard for consequences, in the awareness that God is working in all ways to bring about a better state of affairs and to establish in you His order, wisdom, and joy, will need to be expressed. A new understanding of God as your *real* source of support and happiness will have to fill your mind and heart. A new faith in your own inner spiritual resources, and your ability to bring them to the surface in the things that you need, will have to take the place of negative submissiveness.

Should one always be sweet and forgiving? Yes, but not necessarily soft and without backbone and individual conviction. Be sweet; know it is the expression of Christ ideas in your consciousness. Be forgiving, because the true light reveals the fact that others are only children, experimenting, trying to use what God has given, and dependent to some extent upon the discipline and help which come from bumping up against others. Forgive, because you can see the *real,* and because your forgiveness is the remission of sins, as far as you are concerned—and because it does work mightily to change the individual who falls short.

Forgiveness is not silent consent, the negative appearance of making the best of a situation while underneath there is resentment. Forgiveness is the art of putting something else in place of the thing forgiven. You put the positive realization of the Truth of Being in place of the appearance of negation and adversity which your senses and your intellectual training report. It does not matter that there is no immediate transformation; you have made use of your God power to erase the appearance and to establish Truth. Such an attitude invites only the best from other souls.

If it does not seem that justice is meted out to you, you must know that there is no hindrance to infinite justice. Whether you realize it or not, you may be holding on to the thought that a wrong was done. Your own thoughts and ways must change to conform to the divine plan and law, in which justice is a quality and an active reality. Light of divine understanding and love will show you that no wrong was intended, and no wrong done. You will see the whole matter in a different light, and so your whole being will be flooded with a great love—even gratitude for the good that is to come as a result of the experience of the past.

As you really understand God, you will learn to drop all thought and feeling of anything contrary to good. God is the one Presence and the one Power—the Good omnipotent. The creation is God's and all that God has made is good. We, His children, are made up of His ideas, the qualities of Being.

We in Truth think of ourselves and others as God's children, endeavoring to develop and to use the divine inheritance of faculties and powers implanted by Him. If an individual fails to make wise use of some power, and for the time being disturbs some of our old fixed beliefs or even harms us, we do not stamp his act as a wrong and let such a belief settle back into the subconscious to build up belief in evil and a fear of evil. We simply bless that individual, and realize that he was not yet in the Christ light in the use of the faculties and power which he was exercising at the time. We remind ourselves that while he may have the stature of a man, he is still just a child in his development—at least when he does that which is contrary to spiritual activity.

So long as there is in your subconscious mind (memory and habits of thinking) that which does not chord with Truth (God, Good, the only Presence and Power, in all and through all), you will keep meeting it in some form or other; you will be obliged to keep using the Truth and the power God has given you to change your mind, to cast out the old and to establish a new order.

We must keep remembering that God is Mind, and that man is ever unfolding in his own consciousness the faculties of the one Mind. When this is known, the cities, the people, their habits, their attainments, their wars—all of which outpicture states of mind—will be changed. We should no longer worry about the disposition of those who seem to transgress laws. We should realize that man is always "punished *by* his sins, and not *for* them."

All of man's troubles have come as a result of belief in evil, belief that there are places where God is not, belief that God dwells in a remote heaven and that the earth is very different from His nature. Moses was trying to get his children to transmute the things which they believed to be evil, to lift them up and let the light of God shine upon them. As their faith caused them to lift up their thoughts, they were freed from fear and kept in health, peace, and safety.

We must cease to condemn anything in ourselves, or in the earth. Then, we must recognize life as one Life, and substance as one Substance, and glorify the Father who is the Source of all, in thought and in the very flesh. This we think of as the resurrection and transfiguration. This process goes on day by day, as man awakes and recognizes himself as God's child and seeks to live by his highest Light.

We are not to be too concerned with the appearances of inharmony, lack, and imperfection about us. These things are not real, and they will pass away quickly as Truth takes hold in the consciousness. We are to remember that the Light shines in the dark-

ness—and that in the very midst of the darkness, man's mind opens to the Light, and for
him there is no more darkness.

CONTENTMENT

INSPIRATION, enthusiasm, strength, joy, and outer supply come to you in ever-increasing measure as you depend upon the only Source there is for your sufficiency. As you establish divine order in your thought world within, as you find your home in Christ, the Truth, you are bound to find your right environment— the place that the Father has prepared for you, in which to serve Him and develop your soul.

The only place to find contentment and health is in the place or state of consciousness that Christ, the Truth, has prepared for you. These inner riches do not depend upon outer conditions and we must not bind ourselves by believing that they do. "According to your faith be it done unto you." All of us must hitch our faith to the divine ideas that make for abundance of manifest good. Then we have a foundation upon which to build our castle of health, happiness, and prosperity. The eternal realities upon which to build are discerned by the eyes of faith and spiritual understanding.

So, by finding the all-providing love of God within your own soul, you become a magnet to attract manifest supply to yourself. You become a magnet to attract divine ideas, and your innate wisdom reveals to you how to use these ideas to the best advantage. Your steps are being guided to whatever environment is best for you at this time.

As we bring all our desires into subjection to our wisdom, discrimination, and good judgment, we are not led into detours by blind desires. So, the first thing to do is to bring every desire of the heart into the light of wisdom, to see that what we desire is practical and conducive to our highest good. Thus we are able to go straight to our goal.

"And we know that to them that love God all things work together for good" (Rom. 8:28).

THE CHRIST SPIRIT

Chapter
13

THE SAME CHRIST SPIRIT that was in Jesus is implanted in all children of God. As you find the Christ in yourself, you realize that you are one with Jesus Christ in God-Mind. Your soul has taken deep root in the universal Mind, and you are growing and unfolding, drawing upon the Invisible and making God manifest. The power of Divine Mind is irresistible, and your part is to have faith in it to make its good things manifest in your life and affairs.

The Christ Spirit in you is a magnet to attract the Christ love. And of course, the outer symbols of love and substance are being provided to meet your every need. Realize this Truth: Whatever is your own under the law of good comes to you; whatever does not belong to you is taken away to find its right place.

All true followers of Christ Jesus find that they must continually discipline their thinking and bring it in line with the Truth.

73

Thoughts are formative; they are like seeds that produce after their kind. "As he thinketh within himself, so is he." Thoughts are back of all conversation, so you see that you must co-operate with your Maker by training yourself to think life-giving, health-producing thoughts. Every day during your periods of communion with the Father in the silence, pray for wisdom and guidance. Make yourself open and receptive to the leading of the Spirit. It will be revealed to you just what steps to take in doing your part to establish divine order.

"To him that ordereth his way aright
Will I show the salvation of God."
—Psalms 50:23

There really is no limit to spiritual unfoldment. The Spirit of Truth within your own soul is giving you a right understanding of every experience that comes to you, and you are calling some of your inactive, unused soul powers into expression to meet the need. You are developing your soul, and this is the important thing. The more you exercise your powers the stronger they grow. So, you have the assurance and the satisfaction of knowing that your faith and all the rest of your spiritual faculties are being gradually developed until the Jesus Christ degree of unfoldment is reached.

All new experiences that try your faith are just opportunities for you to make the Good manifest. Best of all, these experiences are the steppingstones upon which you are progressing to more advanced things. They cause you to quicken, awaken, and bring forth into expression more of your innate capabilities that are awaiting your use.

God not only has created the earth, and us, but He is actually the very essence of all that we see about us, and all that is within us. We are free agents; we must learn to take and combine the ideas and the manifest materials into the souls and bodies we are to use.

You see, it isn't that we are doing something by ourselves, and occasionally asking God, outside of us, to help. In reality, God is working out through His offspring that which He has conceived to be the ideal creation and life. But He has given us the power which He is—just as any wise father gives his son full freedom to become the son he feels sure that son will be. The wise father gives his son the best start he knows how to give, then leaves it with the son to use his heritage to make his own way in life. That is just what God is doing with us.

When you truly go to the Christ within yourself, instead of to your own thoughts, you will receive whatever you need. And unless you heed this instruction, drop the unwise things you have been insisting upon, and begin to think of God in you and about you as the total fullness of every good, you will seem to go through an eternity of confusion and lack and hungering. You must direct your prayers up—not up in the skies, but up into God consciousness. When you truly drop thoughts of conditions and personal desires and personalities, and center your attention in God, and think God only, and give thanks that God only is expressing and manifesting everywhere in His universe, then you will speedily dissolve the old error beliefs and their counterparts in the manifest world.

Let me say it again: *Stop* trying so hard to know that everything is as it should be. Just rest your mind and heart and emotions and body in God-Mind. When you are truly thinking God, you cannot struggle to do anything. It is when you are thinking of self that you struggle and see nothing but darkness and grief and failure. No one, not even God, can change you or your circumstances so long as you insist upon looking at and thinking of and worrying about yourself and your problems. Your problems do not exist except in your own mind. And they are there only because you have made them. As soon as you withdraw your thoughts and feelings from the things which you have invited and built up, they will fall flat and dissolve. By abiding in God-Mind (which means perfect order and satisfaction), you will build a new world of peace, joy, wholeness, and success according to the direction of Christ ideas.

There is only one Presence and one Power in earth and the universe: God, the Good, omnipotent. "All authority hath been given unto me [the Christ] in heaven and on earth" (Mt. 28:18). Remember this: whatever you have done, whatever you contemplate, you are learning lessons, growing, and going forward to a day of light, joy, and freedom.

The solution of your every problem lies with you and the Father. Others cannot tell you what to do. Others cannot keep you from doing that which is best. As you consecrate yourself to God and seek earnestly and persistently and patiently to do His good will, you will find that real peace, strength, freedom, and wisdom are yours. The Mind of God, active in your consciousness, is your present help. If you turn to God and away from human reasoning, longing, and fears, he will show you the way that leads to the fullness of your good.

The really important thing, you know, is to lift your consciousness above the things of the material world—above personality and human limitations and unfold your Christ consciousness. Instead of letting the mind dwell on people and seeing them as personalities, the follower of Jesus Christ should keep his attention upon universal Truth, and gradually lift all his thinking to the Truth standard.

Thinking habitually about people, their actions, their human limitations, tends to bind one to personal consciousness. To do the great works that Jesus promised His followers would do, one must raise his consciousness to the place where he is able to see the perfect image and likeness of God in all people. One must not let himself be influenced by the likes and dislikes of the human nature. Christ is the real Self of each individual. By seeing only the Christ in all people, we not only strengthen our own spiritual consciousness but help all whom we contact to realize and express their innate divinity.

SPIRITUAL UNDERSTANDING

IF YOU WOULD GROW in understanding of spiritual things, become as a little child and let the universal Spirit of Good teach you. Do not strain your intellect in trying to understand the mighty questions of life; wait until you have developed faculties which can comprehend them. There is a running to and fro among men that will never cease so long as they try to explain spiritual things with the intellect. Listen to the stillness within your own soul—and you will find it resonant with a new tongue.

The world lacks spiritual understanding. All about us are those who preach and teach the so-called religion and doctrine of Jesus Christ, yet how few there are who have the understanding of *reality* which He promised will come to those who believe. It is quite evident that they do not have the understanding of His teaching that leads to the "signs" mentioned in the last chapter of Mark as bearing witness of those who believe.

It is found, in the study of Truth, that these signs do follow those who get the spiritual understanding which comes with a full acceptance of spiritual science. A partial understanding is accompanied by a manifestation of a part of the signs. Even a slight spiritual perception leads to the unfoldment in many people of the power to heal the sick. This is being demonstrated all over the land. It is becoming so common that on every hand "infants" in spiritual understanding are now doing mighty works in bringing health to invalids.

This understanding, however, is not the full-orbed sun which it is promised shall be found in those who have put on the white raiment of purity; it is simply a few straggling rays that have found their way through the shifting rifts of mortal beliefs. Healing these perishing bodies of the world of shadows is not the ultimate of Truth; nor is it even a factor in the future glories of the permanent unfoldment which will surely be the portion of those who come into full understanding. These sick and diseased bodies are results of flagrant errors that men have made in their attempts to solve the problem of life without divine help.

These errors can be corrected. There are many now on the road to an understanding that will eradicate the belief in death so completely that their bodies will never pass through the state of physical corruption. Eventually their understanding of spiritual things will so refine the physical body that it will fade from the view of those in whom the real has not been likewise perceived. This process will in time become so common that all will look forward to it as the ultimate, and dying in the old way will be thought disgraceful.

Those who fade out of sight will not necessarily go anywhere as we understand distance, but will simply come into a fuller understanding of the new heaven and the new earth which are now right here about us. Had we the understanding of spiritual things which is ours by divine right, we would see that we now touch elbows with the inhabitants of a realm beautiful beyond comparison. This planet is in reality a thought of Divine Mind and it is alive with the same vivifying intelligence that animates man. Its *real Self* is spiritual and corresponds to the Christ principle, which is the life of man. It is the habitation of the perfected souls that have come into a consciousness of their unity with the one Mind, and as we go within ourselves in the silence we come into a certain degree of harmony with it. It is what Jesus spoke of as the heaven that is within you.

Thus, the new heaven and the new earth which are promised will not involve another creation but simply a rolling up, as a scroll, of the erroneous concepts of men as to the reality of things all about them. Those whose spiritual understanding is restored to them can now and here enjoy this new Jerusalem. It is simply knowing the *real* from the unreal. When man knows this he is already in heaven, no matter what his external condition may indicate.

The full understanding that is now dawning will do away with all the inverted images—sin, sickness, sorrow, and death—which have been invested by men with apparent permanency. These are not in any sense real, but are wrong combinations in which the senses have arranged their little store of knowledge.

A harmonious relation of mental concepts would change the earth and all its relations in the twinkling of an eye. No change in reality would take place—simply an adjustment of the thoughts now held by men. For instance, it took people a long time to comprehend that the sun did not go around the earth. Our senses evidence conclusively that the sun does go around the earth. But we now see with the mind's eye just how the earth and the planets travel around the sun, and an entirely new relation of things presents itself. We see that right here within sight of our eyes, upon which we depend for information, exists a condition of affairs of which our eyes tell us nothing—which, in fact, they flatly contradict.

When you think of this earth and all that is upon it as being made of the very substance of God, and always under His divine law, you will no longer be disturbed by things going on about you. You will rest every night, and your days will be pleasant.

Don't bother about what others may think or say about you. God loves you, and approves of what you do when you are doing your best to follow the Jesus Christ way. The opinions of others cannot get you down or lift you up. You have the power of God within you to raise yourself up to where you know you are His child, with ability along all lines and with freedom to do whatever you really wish to do.

God is helping you now to know that this is the Truth. God is showing you that your best dreams are coming true; that you are to forget the past and its disappointments; that you are to do everything as though you were doing it for God. God is a great, loving Father, Who is interested in you, and Who can and will help you. He will supply your needs, and will show you how to keep happy and healthy.

You cannot hope for peace and joy and health and plenty and opportunity for greater development as long as your subconscious mind is weighted down with old burdens. When you desire with all your heart to live the life God has planned for His children, the life that is revealed in the indwelling Christ mind, you will find old beliefs and habits crumbling, and you will face the necessity for building a new faith. Just as Jesus met the old race beliefs in sorrow and suffering and death, and rose triumphant out of them, so you have the light and power to meet the race beliefs in sorrow and lack and failure and death, and to rise out of them in the true Christ consciousness of life.

Your own willingness to come into spiritual consciousness and to develop and use the Christ power will determine your growth. But you are to keep to the Holy Spirit as your light and to let the study of the writings of others, or their lives, be but witnesses to you of what God ideas can do. Others may be instrumental in calling forth into activity the power within you. The Holy Spirit is the activity of God-Mind in the consciousness of man.

The long way, the most difficult way, back to the Father's house is the way of experience. The shortcut is in being receptive and obedient to the leading of the Holy Spirit in thought, word, and deed, putting God first in your life.

When you come into a spiritual realization, as you do in the silence, expect it to go down into the depths of your body consciousness and do its powerful and perfect work. None of us has learned to abide in the Christ consciousness continuously, but the times we do rise into it keep us growing and overcoming and establishing more and more of its Truth in our lives.

We are not to feel discouraged if, after such a glorious experience, we seem to lose the Christ consciousness and go back into the old habits. We cannot really lose anything that Spirit has expressed in us. We simply let it sink into our human consciousness to do its good work, just as we plant seeds in the ground and apparently lose them in order that they may grow and bring forth many, many other seeds, and the beauty and fragrance of the budding and blossoming which come before the ripe fruit. The Holy Spirit of Jesus Christ has sown in us the seeds of light and health and prosperity, seeds of the Father's creating. These seeds are working in us to transform us completely. That which has quickened our souls and given us the joyous sense of freedom will work in every cell of our bodies to give them that same wonderful sense of wholeness and freedom.

At times the soul will reveal to us conditions that are wholly at variance with the reports of the senses and intellect, yet more real and substantial than any of these. Hence, if you would know the perfect relation of all things in the universe, cultivate the soul. It is Intelligence Itself and will reveal to you, in the silence of meditation, glories and beauties of which you have not dreamed. It will show you that your supposed condition of sickness is simply a false adjustment of thought, and if you listen to its promptings it will bring to you health and harmony in all your relations. All things move from center to periphery, and man is no exception. Find the law of your center and the periphery will be regulated in exact proportion to the degree with which you allow that center to express itself.

Chapter 15

THE SECRET PLACE OF SPIRIT

WE ARE ON THE threshold of a new heaven and a new earth—a new consciousness. John the Baptist came to herald Jesus Christ. He said, "Repent ye; for the kingdom of heaven is at hand" (Mt. 3:2). We know more than the people of that day understood about the kingdom of heaven. We are turning from the world of the outer and are coming into the wonderful place which is called "the secret place of the Most High" (Ps. 91:1). Jesus Christ called this place the "inner chamber." He said, "When thou prayest, enter into thine inner chamber, and having shut thy door, pray to thy Father who is in secret" (Mt. 6:6). We do this in the consciousness of the Father's presence within. As we enter, we close the doors of the outer senses and get away from the whirl of material activities. We feel a divine calmness; we gain understanding of ourselves.

Let us take this affirmation to help us realize the Christ consciousness: *God's perfect idea in me is now building a perfect body, and I am satisfied.* As the little germ in the seed brings forth its kind, so in each human being is put the divine image and likeness, the potentiality of bringing forth perfection in mind, body, and affairs. Jesus Christ is our example of perfection. He was the first to teach of the new birth, the new growth of mankind. In order to be satisfied we first must have the perfect idea and then the perfect body.

We are longing to bring into manifestation that which has been given us to bring forth; that is why we are sometimes restless and discontented. That which the world has to give does not satisfy, but when we go into the secret place, when we learn to be still and to know the I AM (God's perfect Idea of us), we lack nothing. We can become like Jesus Christ if we abide in the secret place of Spirit.

The silence is a kind of stillness, a place of retreat into which we may enter and, having entered, may know the Truth. We go into the silence by observing the instructions, "Be still, and know" (Ps. 46:10). The only way really to *know* is to become perfectly still, to get away from the outer and from looking for things, into the inner quiet where we are alone with wisdom. In the silence, wisdom is given for every need.

In the outer we are always trying to get pleasure from things. We call it pleasure; it is pleasure momentarily, but it does not last.

The pleasures of sense gratify for a little while, but after the pleasures are over we feel bereft and empty. Outer pleasure is like moonlight: Sometimes it is very beautiful, but there is no element of growth in it. It does not help the power within us to come forth.

The silence is like the sun: it is always shining. It brings forth the best that is within us, the image and likeness of God that is waiting to be brought into activity, that will show itself after the fashion that God intended it should.

In the silence we get the wonderful inward joy that is of God. We see what the *real* is. Those who seek pleasure in the outer are in reality seeking eternal joy: the joy that no man can take away, the joy that Jesus Christ promised us, the joy that comes when we know what it means to be a child of God, when we know what the Father would have us know.

To help us forego outer pleasure for the inner joy, let us take a fitting word for meditation. Let us become willing to sacrifice the pleasures of the senses that are fleeting and unsatisfying; let us be willing to relinquish outer pleasures for the joy of Spirit—the consciousness of the presence of the Father. Let us take this statement for meditation: *I am willing to sacrifice the pleasures of sense that I may enter into the joys of Spirit.*

In sacrificing the pleasures of sense for the

joys of Spirit, you are not depriving yourself of pleasures; you are exchanging the moonlight for the great glory of the sun. Jesus said, "The spirit indeed is willing, but the flesh is weak" (Mt. 26:41). The flesh can say nothing when Spirit decides; the flesh has no power, no profit in itself. It is Spirit that quickens.

Unity of Spirit conquers the world for the Lord. We are sending forth peace to every land. Nations will forget to fight if we continue to know that all people express the one Life.

No one will deny that God is omnipresent or that God is all, yet we talk about a great many presences, a great many powers, and other things that do not belong to God. No one denies Good. All persons seek after it when they know how. When we find that there is only one Presence, the real Presence of infinite Goodness, we find no place for the opposite quality.

When we recognize the one Presence, we eliminate the many presences. One of our great scientists says that he never found God until he found Him in his laboratory. He says that he looked upon the world and saw many different things that were called God, many different powers that were called God, but he himself did not find God. However, in the laboratory many things that he tested in his crucible went into the invisible. He had a name for this invisible product; he called it the ether. He found that ether has intelligence and power, and that the different forms in nature are the garments with which God clothes Himself. We are learning the law by which we bring forth from invisible Substance. We like to think that we can deal with it as God dealt with it. We bring it forth according to our thoughts, making of it different forms and shapes, making our worlds according to our ideas. But the great pattern which God gave is unchanged; it is revealed to us through Jesus Christ. We are to work by that pattern, to bring forth the life idea that Jesus Christ brought forth. We may feel confused by the manifold activities in the world, yet there is only one impulse back of them all. When we get so still that the One becomes visible to us, then we see our own Christ within. Truly, we know that there is only one Power, one Presence, one Wisdom.

Chapter 16

THE
OVERCOMING
OF FEAR

SOMETIMES we fear that we have not the ability to do a thing we ought to do; we fear that there are obstacles in the way. If there *are* obstacles, we have made them. God never put anything in the way of progress. When we get rid of our fears, we find that the way is clear for us to go the Lord's way.

David said, "I will fear no evil; for thou art with me" (Ps. 23:4). He spoke these words from a consciousness that was filled with the knowledge and the power of God. As a boy he was a keeper of the sheep. He was fearless when the lions and the wolves came to take the sheep. He had a sling, as many boys have, but he used it defensively instead of aggressively, and he practiced with it until he was efficient and fearless.

There came a great emergency, when David's people stood in fear and trembling—afraid not of the Philistine army but of the great giant who came out and taunted the Israelites—a symbol of the giant that no man, in his own strength, is able to conquer. When the boy David came into the camp of the Israelitish army, he saw the condition of things at once. He saw that there was only one remedy. He went to meet the giant. He said, "I come to thee in the name of Jehovah of hosts, the God of the armies of Israel, whom thou hast defied" (1 Sam. 17:45). With his usual weapon, the sling, he was a laughingstock to the giant who stood there sure of his own power—but the giant fell before David. David was fearless because he relied on the power of God and had something with which he could always hit the mark. What the armies of Israel could not accomplish, he brought about in the name of the Lord.

Probably each of us has to face some particular danger, one that is greater than all the rest of the ills that hinder him. If he *knows* and is faithful to Truth, he need never fear. Whatever troubles may seem to arise, he can meet them with Truth. Nothing can stand before it.

If you would overcome all your enemies and find your freedom, you must be true to your one defense. There is only one Power and one Presence—the Good. All scheming and falsity must fall before the consciousness that there is only one power—God. The power of darkness will vanish before it.

Let us make these thoughts a part of our consciousness: *I cannot be afraid, for God is* omnipresent Good. God is omnipresent protection. "I will fear no evil; for thou art with me."

THE
LONGING
OF OUR SOULS

GREAT UNREST comes from a lack of holiness. We seem to be divided into fractions and sections; we give one part of our minds to one thing and another part of our minds to another. And always within us is a longing for something higher, an unrest, because we are not satisfied with life as it seems to us. The Psalmist conceived the right idea of life in its fullness and completeness when he said, "I shall be satisfied, when I awake, with thy likeness" (Ps. 17:15 KJV). That likeness now slumbers in us as the seed in the earth; it is the something that is always urging us to better things. It is that within us which wants something more than the outer activities of life. We never shall be satisfied until we find ourselves. It is this restlessness that accounts for all the error we find in the outer.

Our restlessness represents a power that is crying out to be expressed. It may take the form of appetite or of ambition, but rightly directed it will be a wonderful something within us that will transcend all the desires of the outer senses. When our powers are placed aright, we shall direct our aspirations and ambitions toward God; we shall know that we can be satisfied with nothing that earth can give. Just think what the Christ life will mean to us when we let it take charge of our consciousness.

We do not have to stimulate our senses to bring us anything; it is already ours. So, let us see whether we cannot really find out what our souls are longing for.

We condemn men for drinking liquor, but we should not do so. The drinker has a great longing to do something. He does not want to follow the common walks of life; he wants to follow the higher ways. Not understanding this urge within himself, he thinks that he can satisfy it with sense, so he takes something stimulating. We are never satisfied through sense; it enslaves us more and more. Aspiration is the soul's trying to find its wings, trying to realize wholeness in Christ. Never, until we find wholeness in Christ, shall we be satisfied.

Those who give way to appetite, who drink liquor, who take drugs, are hungering and thirsting after righteousness. Remember the Jesus Christ words of light and blessing, "Blessed are they that hunger and thirst after righteousness: for they shall be filled." In most cases, an individual who drinks too much is an unusual soul, a soul who has developed some of his faculties and powers until he is very sensitive. He longs for the perfect balance to enable him to express rightly these powers that he feels but does not know how to express.

First of all, drop out of your mind the idea that a bad habit is a terrible thing. When you think of it as a terrible and powerful thing, you keep giving it as much or more power than you allow the Christ. The drink-craving habit is not a moral shortcoming; it is a crying out of some of the tissue masses of the body, and an effort of the body to meet the needs of the soul for satisfying mental and physical food.

Sometimes we fail to know the needs of growing children, or of grownups, and these persons go on year after year, failing to meet the demands of the cell tissues. Their bodies are hungry, starved, and often filled with substance they cannot use. Sometimes they are inflamed by the frequent eating of foods highly seasoned, or foods otherwise unsuited to the body's needs. Sometimes people grow up with habits of eating certain kinds of foods that are easy to get and taste good but still have not the vital life elements in them that are required by the blood and the nerves. Those who feel free to indulge in some sort of stimulant sometimes become victims of bad habits. Others hold out against this, but their health is broken, and they turn to medicine. Others will get their alcohol and its effects through foods which are considered harmless but which contain the same constituent elements as alcohol.

In dealing with these things, we reach the individual by instructing him as to the Truth of his being. Then we hold him in this consciousness and seek to show him how he has unknowingly made unwise use of his life and the substance which is provided for his nourishment.

A belief in some sort of repression and lack, and the consequent sense of lack of life, cause a soul hungering and also a physical hungering for food. Intemperate eating is accompanied by a craving for stimulants. Those who prepare and serve meals without knowledge of the body's real needs are often the outer cause of the development of the drinking habit.

A strong desire for a fuller realization of life sometimes leads to the use of stimulants. When someone who is near to the drinker comes to his senses and looks Godward, the way to freedom and wholeness and real satisfaction is revealed.

The first step in healing another's physical weakness and tendency to drunkenness is to give up all grief and worry, and to withdraw all condemnation and censure—for the liquor, for those who serve it, and for the individual who takes it. Let the same divine love of God which Jesus described in His story of the prodigal son fill mind and heart and flow out to all concerned. When we love, and pour out the subtle love essence which stirs the heart center, we are moving to action the life energies of Being, and a great law of mind equilibrium is fulfilled. We need to help these children of God to know how to center their love upon Him and His qualities in themselves and those about them. We have not known how to help our children to recognize and unfold the fullness of their God-given resources and faculties and powers. When they come to us they are "bundles" of receptivity and undeveloped faculties and desires; they absorb almost anything we hand out to them—even things we are not aware of impressing them with. Then we are dismayed when their efforts are unwisely directed.

So, let us go to the Source of all help, all life, all supply, and all opportunity, and build up the consciousness of health and plenty. Instead of struggling in an outer way, let us go within and build a foundation for real success and prosperity and satisfaction.

Use affirmations similar to the following for the purpose of setting your mind in order and setting into action the thought causes which will bring the desired results:

I, too, will arise and go to my Father and receive His love and wisdom and blessing. I now behold His kingdom, His riches, and His unfailing life pouring through me and manifesting for all my needs.

YOUR
WONDERFUL
BODY

SPIRIT IS ALL. We are to bring the soul and the body into the Christ consciousness—the right use of all that God gives. Where would you draw the line between Spirit and the material, when there is no evidence that God has placed such boundaries? We see Spirit manifesting in the flesh, in the centers of consciousness, and in the organs of the body as expressions of energy and substance. If we make a separation in our consciousness, we shall have something that we do not know how to deal with. We are working with vital spiritual qualities, and we shall change the character of their manifestations as our growth makes change desirable and necessary.

Let God carry out His will and way in you now. He needs your temple for the uses of His Spirit, in bringing His kingdom into the earth. It *is* His temple, you know, and you have no right to think anything short of perfection about it. Begin this moment to use every ounce of energy and intelligence you have for God, and you will find that you will keep drawing more and more deeply from the wellsprings of His life and love. Your body will become the "living sacrifice, holy, acceptable to God, which is your spiritual service" (Rom. 12:1).

The body is like a child. It needs constant prompting and training and discipline and praise and appreciation. Your body needs your attention, your love, your training.

Give all your thought and your love and your determination to perfecting your body. Look at that wonderful body temple. It is precious to you. Begin to see that body the instrument of the soul, which enables you to carry out God's plans in the earth.

You have everything you need to enable you to do the many things you came into the world to do, but you need to let the Spirit of God take hold of your soul and set it to doing its perfect work in the body. This will require the exercise of good, common sense. Look at your chest: it breathes in the very breath of God's life; God is flowing through it to supply all your needs. Look at your limbs and feet: God has created them to enable you to walk on the earth (which He created for you) and to move about freely and to do that which gives you practical knowledge of the laws governing life on this plane. Look at your arms and hands: they are God's, and He has continued to dwell in them and sustain them all during these years. Your head is wonderfully poised, so that you may look about and see the beauty and power and life and light of God manifested in His creation everywhere. After contemplating the wonders of your physical body temple and feeling the stirring of the new life which your thoughts will send coursing through you, think again, just as happily and intently, about the mental activities which must depend upon these centers in the body for their success. Let your body know the joy of your loving attention and interest; give it the exercise it needs.

Perhaps long ago you conceived the idea that you could reach heaven only without your flesh. You may have had the early-day church belief that the body is dust and that it must be humiliated and neglected if the soul is to be truly loyal to Christ and prepared for entrance into glory. Such notions are not true to Jesus Christ's teachings. They do more to tear down the soul and body than the so-called sins of this world.

So, just make up your mind that you are not going to worry about "overcoming." You are just going to let the life and strength of God flow through you. God has bestowed his gifts upon you with the idea of your using them freely, here and now. You can do whatever you really want to do—but you will have to want it enough actually to make the effort to do it. If you want to glorify God in actually living the happy, healthy, everyday life He has wisely planned for you, you will do it. The Spirit of God in you is willing. But you must demand of the flesh that it obey the Spirit.

Study to renew your subconsciousness. Wherever a race belief has gotten hold, or an error concept has tried to work out, go to work with the Truth. Whatever change you make mentally and purposefully will begin at once to change every part of your life.

Then add to this spiritual treatment careful attention to your living habits. Bathe with the idea of opening all the millions of little doors of the skin to let out the used-up materials and to let in the sunshine and its energy. Eat with the understanding that you are providing God-given materials which the inner Intelligence will use to nourish and cleanse and renew all of your body every day. There are foods for the muscle tissues, others for the blood, others for the glands, others for skin and hair and nails and brain and eyes.

The time will come when we can draw forth from the universal mind-stuff just the elements we need, in their right proportion and relation, to maintain the proper balance in our whole organism. The time will come, I am confident, when we shall be able to draw chemical substance from the fourth dimensional realm down into our physical bodies. But in the meantime we need to make practical the knowledge we have concerning bodily renewal, through using intelligence and discrimination, particularly in the selection of our food.

Perhaps you think that it would be too tedious a job to learn all about the body and its needs. But once you begin to think about it, it becomes a fascinating game to learn to discern your body's hunger and to satisfy it, physically as well as spiritually.

Everything in God's world is working toward perfection. The restoring power of God in the midst of you is working quickly and harmoniously to build in cells and substance that will knit together whatever place needs rebuilding.

When the harshness of others seems to crush you, you can send forth love, the power that not only blesses you but goes forth to redeem the adverse conditions in the outer. When petals of the fragrant rose are crushed by cruel hands they send forth their sweetness even more than before. "Love therefore is the fulfilment of the law" (Rom. 13:10). The law of God in your heart keeps you sweet always.

You may give up, this very moment, all resentment, all dread, and all questioning as to the future. For you are not obliged to continue living without the perfect use of all your functions and organs and members. Afflictions of all kinds exist primarily in the realm of mind, and have been caused by some failure of the mind to receive and understand and express the Christ ideas which God gives. Then, there is usually another cause: the mind directing the physical functions in the effort to avoid undesirable experiences, to shut out that which the soul feels is not for it, or to grasp and make use of something it wants and does not know how to gain in the divinely appointed way. The mind not only directs the faculties in their expression and takes account of these things about one; it actually is the means of constructing and reconstructing the physical organism.

You, as an individual soul, took up your expression as a living being to embody in consciousness and experience that which we think of as God's image-likeness man. In other words, you are a child of God, an offspring, an expression and combination of God Ideas or qualities of being. Your own soul desired a vehicle of expression, and through the use of the creative law of life you came in touch with those who helped you to build the physical body temple. Your own soul's choice drew you to those who were in tune with your soul's desires and expressions.

Body help comes, not in forgetting the things that were but in getting a different viewpoint, seeing back of the experiences themselves, and lifting one's vision to behold

God—the divine Father-Mother to which the soul is ever united and from which one may constantly draw light, strength, love, substance, and life.

Because you came into a new body, and because your soul was obliged to make adjustments to accommodate itself to the conditions and persons about it, you may sometimes be unable to hold steadfastly to the light which your soul should receive from God-Mind and which it should use in its unfoldment.

Every experience will prove encouraging to you when you begin to understand it, for it will show you that the mind is powerful and that the body and its functions respond readily and fully to the bidding of the mind. So, you see, healing is always assured!

You are not to turn your mind and heart away from people and try to content yourself without a full, free expression of love and interest in others. This will be a great help to you in unfolding your spiritual consciousness and in bringing your body into perfection. Do not admit limitations as any part of you—they are just results of temporary mistakes. The way in which Truth will direct you lacks nothing of love, peace, joy, beauty, and well-rounded self-expression. Perhaps you do not do just as you had formerly dreamed you would, but the things that your clearer spiritual vision and your better use of your faculties and powers will prompt you to do will be even better and more satisfying and worth while.

Study and practice daily, keeping your mind and heart, your vision and your emotions fixed on God—God in you. "Christ in you" is your "hope of glory." Christ is God's perfect pattern of His own son in you. There is no *real* satisfaction apart from the interpretation of this Christ Self in daily living. You are a soul who has come with a rich spiritual development. The very fact that you try to close out the undesirable things, that you love and take a great interest in your fellow man, and that you want to accomplish much, proves that you are ready to awaken to the Christ Light—in which you will understand that there is really only one Presence and Power: omnipotent Good. All things are possible with you because you are here to let God express through you His own perfect plan of life.

When there is a sense of feeling lost, it is but the result of impressions received from without, from error thoughts and false convictions "wished on you" by the race beliefs and your own immature use of the senses and mental faculties. You are not lost! You are in your right place in the Father-Mind this moment. Look, then, to God-Mind, with faith, and you will begin to see the Light. Keep your gaze upon the Light and you cannot possibly see any darkness. When you are looking toward the Light, shadows fall behind you. The Light is within you, and as you learn to look within, you become radiant, because Light is a quality of Mj117ind and its essence is finding outlets through your mental faculties.

With Christ light flooding your soul, you see causes and effects correctly, and you behold the great Cause (God) in which are your perfection and freedom. This is the *real* healing for soul and body.

Make up your mind that you are going to see God everywhere, and you will begin to discern the God qualities expressing in everyone and everything, however imperfectly. Be determined to listen for and hear God's voice and the radiation of God's power and love, and the sounds that once disturbed will not affect you. Instead they will impress you with the fact that God's life and power and love are in everything and are seeking expression.

Chapter 19

Spiritual Control

OUR RELIGIOUS LIFE, heretofore, has led us to feel that our thoughts and our emotions were all that were necessary to our spiritual experience. The body of man was disregarded, considered as of little consequence and thought to be unresponsive to the finer things of Spirit.

A thing is not less spiritual because it has taken form, weight, and color. That which might be termed material is a misconception, an unwise combination of thoughts and elements that produces an undesirable result. Spirit becomes manifest in man's expression of what God gives.

Unity emphasizes the need for control of the physical by the spiritual. But many of the things that we do, and expect to control, are not at all spiritual (in the sense that they are in accord with God's laws and plans). The real control is in living according to the perfect pattern and law. It is not spiritual thought that prompts one to abuse the body in any way. It is not spiritual thought or desire that allows one to eat when there is no need for food, or to partake of elements of food which are not what the body requires at the time. It is not spiritual thought that causes one to worry, to become tense, or to drive the body in the effort to gain intellectually.

Evidently the individual soul has felt the need of just such an earth home as the body temple. We are taking it that the body, free from the inharmonies and weaknesses imposed upon it through errors, is a part of God's plan of life. We understand man to be a threefold being. Just now we are convinced that the regular appropriation of certain manifest life elements is required to maintain the body at a given rate of vibration—which we know as health, endurance, and ability to transmit thought into action. We do not know how long such a plan will be in effect, and we are not greatly concerned about the matter. But it is reasonable to suppose that we shall not learn a great deal about higher laws and manifestations until we have learned to live by these present laws. When we can sustain the body in health, activity, and radiance indefinitely, we shall have gained a better understanding of the true purpose of life and shall be ready to enter upon a mode of living that may free us from the observance of laws we term "physical."

The science of building and operating an airplane would not permit the builder and the mechanic to build the machine out of just any materials or to drive it with just any fuel. We know that the power to build and to drive the machine is in the builder's mind and in the universal atmosphere. Nevertheless, knowing this and acting upon it, we do not seek to set aside the laws revealed by Intelligence in constructing and operating the machine.

Man learns to build an airplane in which to fly, before he is entrusted with the higher law of taking his body through the air without a manifest vehicle. To build the plane and use it and observe the laws governing its flight is not denying God's spiritual laws. It is leading man forward to the discovery of greater things.

So it is with maintaining ourselves in health, and in studying and applying spiritual rules of action. We must learn to make the right use of what we have. Having done this, we shall find ourselves in possession of more.

Since the soul is consciousness, it is reasonable to assume that it is aware of all that really interests it and all that it desires to identify itself with. One who had been spiritually awake and active in soul and body would not be likely to "fall asleep" even though the body were for some reason given up. Such a one would be on the alert to satisfy his soul hunger and to appreciate all that he could experience without the flesh and the physical structure which his centers of consciousness had built.

The soul which is obedient to the spiritual laws as they relate it to others, would not weaken the body and give it up. In the event that its shortcomings did wear out this body, or sever all connection with it, the soul would bide its time and await the right opportunity for its re-embodiment.

If there are to be other and different experiences, Spirit will make it known to the soul. Devotion to that which is highest and best, without neglect of the physical, will result in the awakening, which will give light and peace and freedom to help the soul to go forward fearlessly.

Chapter 20

CREATURE OF HABIT

THE BODY is a creature of habit. Without the positive, purposeful daily effort of the mind, it becomes after a time difficult to break the habits into which it has plunged. In the mind there is some negative idea concerning life which has resulted in the soul's giving up and allowing the body to slump and refuse to do the things for which it has been formed and sustained. The body becomes lazy and does not want even to move about. But once the mind takes up a definite program and stirs up interest in things worth while here and now, the body will begin to wake up and to draw the abundant life of Spirit down into the various nerve centers, bones, muscles, and organs. New energy will flow through the organism and the soul will eagerly use it in setting about the work of releasing energy into the flesh to accomplish the necessary work of healing.

Years of negative thinking and inactivity may cause the body to lose its ability to get up and walk about and do the many things for which it is created. The individual has to train the body persistently to do that which he wishes. Use of the organs, muscles, and members will restore them to normal. The very fact that individuals have stayed alive through years of lying in bed is proof that a certain amount of the life and substance of God has been received and appropriated by the body. But when the body sets up fixed, negative, limited habits, it just stays in bed and fails to use the perfect Christ pattern for its renewal and action.

The glorious Truth of Being transforms mind and body. Those who are transformed will arise and take up their beds and walk. They will begin to glorify God in doing the things that are well-pleasing in His sight. They will know that life is eternal and inexhaustible.

Through the right use of God-given power, a person may make his life the very thing he most wants.

Chapter 21

THE HEALTHY CHANNEL

THERE IS no reason why the machinery in our body temples should wear out, because the Creator is still on the job, building up and renewing His temples to the extent that we permit. When we co-operate by thinking habitually in terms of eternal life, eternal youth, ever-increasing strength, and perfect health, we are renewed moment by moment.

God wants all of us to manifest His life, His radiant, glowing health, His joy—in fact, all that He is. The Creator is now breathing His purifying, vitalizing, cleansing breath of life into each cell and fiber of your body, filling you with strength that is a barrier to any and every appearance of negativeness.

Do not let belief in time enter into the demonstration. If you have faith that the healing will take place right now, why, "according to your faith be it done unto you." "Behold, I will bring . . . health and cure, and I will cure them; and I will reveal unto them abundance of peace and truth" (Jer. 33:6).

The power that created you is always at work to restore you and to maintain you in wholeness. Now that you are coming into the understanding of Christ principles and learning how to co-operate with your indwelling Lord and Healer, you are made whole and well in every part.

Do not let the opinion of any doctor cause you to waver in the least. God is the health of His people, and He is your health. "Be still, and know that I am God" (Ps. 46:10). "I am the Lord that healeth thee" (Ex. 15:26 KJV).

Pray for your innate and unlimited faith in God to be quickened and stirred into positive action. With your eye of faith see yourself continuously manifesting purity, harmony, and wholeness in every part of your body.

Jesus said, "All things, whatsoever ye shall ask in prayer, believing, ye shall receive " (Mt. 21:22). Learn to give thanks in the realization that you are already healed.

Think of your organism as being the pure Life and Substance of Spirit made manifest. Keep your mind filled with joyous, constructive, beautiful, health-producing thoughts that maintain harmony in both mind and body. When your mind is peaceful the healing energies flow through your whole being freely and abundantly.

Instead of looking at any appearance of inharmony, keep your attention centered upon the healing Presence and Power of

"Christ in you." You are then strengthened, and faith is manifested as the very "assurance of things hoped for, a conviction of things not seen" (Heb. 11:1). "Thy healing shall spring forth speedily" (Is. 58:8).

Some physiologists who keep careful watch of the ways of the body believe that we are renewed bodily about every nine months. Why should flesh age when it is renewed so often? It must be that the old molds of the mortal mind and the thoughts that belong to it need to be remodeled, and the remedy is, "Be ye transformed by the renewing of your mind" (Rom. 12:2).

The wonderful principles that Jesus used in performing His so-called miracles are working here and now for all those who have faith in God as the source of their blessings and who are making the teachings of the Master practical in their daily thinking and living. "God is no respecter of persons."

It is all a matter of consciousness, and when we unfold our fourth-dimensional consciousness we shall see into Omnipresence, and there will be nothing hidden from us. When we refine and spiritualize our consciousness and the temple in and through which it finds expression, we shall be able to think of the most distant point in the universe, and immediately be there. There is no time or space to one who has unfolded the Christ consciousness to the degree that Jesus had.

Mind is omnipresent, and it is through letting the same Mind that is in Christ Jesus be in us that we transcend the limitations of the material mind.

What a mighty uplift we experience by repeating His holy name in the silence! As we see Christ in our flesh and realize the oneness of our Spirit, soul, and body in Christ, our bodies will share in the freedom and uplift. New understanding will gradually come, and many wonderful, undiscovered laws will be understood as fast as we develop the capacity to know and use them righteously.

The man who believes in materiality and looks to sense consciousness for satisfaction is clothed in garments of darkness. Every thought has life and substance. When we think about material things and conditions as being real and having power, we give them the life and substance of our thought. When we give our attention to sense consciousness, which deals with material things, we build up the sense man in ourselves; he takes the essence of our souls for himself to the extent that we let our thoughts dwell on things apart from God, the Source.

We are learning to think about Truth principles, and as the carnal states of mind pass, we are profiting in small ways through the wisdom gained of experience.

Whatever is Good is permanent and enduring; it cannot be lost or destroyed. We refer to spiritual values when we make this statement. Even the sense consciousness is good in its way, however; it serves a purpose. Whatever is Good in it endures and remains part of the spiritual soul in us.

Your Christ Self has an infinite capacity for expression along spiritual lines. Your I AM consciousness is taking an active part in the work of redemption and regeneration that is going forward in you. The ragged garments of material thought, the thoughts that deal with externals and personality, are being denied and discarded to the degree that you give the energy and substance of your mind to spiritual thinking.

Clothe your mind with the garments of Truth, and let your thoughts yield to you their wealth of spiritual power. Think from the Truth standpoint when you think about the outer, material world. It is by your spiritual thinking that you build up your spiritual consciousness.

The eyes are the physical organs which are the outpicturing of the capacity of the mind to discern—mentally, physically, spiritually— all that is. Seeing is a mental process and the eyes are the instruments which register what the mind has been trained to think and to behold. When your mental processes are in perfectly harmonious accord with the ideas of

Divine Mind, your sight is perfect and your eyes function properly with nothing to hinder.

Your nose is the physical organ which is the outpicturing of the detective capacity of the mind. The sense of smell is also mental in reality. The sense itself enables the mind to function in its capacity to find that which is good for the soul and body, and to direct the individual toward appropriation of it. The mind which is in tune with the true Being, the Christ Self, is not interested in ferreting out evil or in dwelling upon the undesirable in any way. The mind which is expressing the Good and the True does not think adverse thoughts or believe in impurity of any sort in the self or in others. So, this sense of smell is a power of God-Mind, which is ever working to connect you with your good.

Seeing, hearing, smelling, tasting, feeling, intuition, and the power to identify yourself with the Absolute (God, the Good) are all faculties that work in the realm of mind, but all have their physical side as well. That which you think—of yourself, or of others, or of the creation in general—you build up a belief in and begin to register in your own soul and body. That which you habitually see mentally, your eyes begin to visualize, and the cell structures of the organs themselves are affected and built according to the vibrations set up by the thoughts. This is true of other senses and their organs, also.

Chapter 22

No
Incurable
Condition

THERE IS no such thing as an incurable "disease" in the body. The activities, weaknesses, and abnormalities to which the medical profession gives names are but the efforts of the God-given inner Intelligence to deal with conditions that the individual has produced by his failure to understand the Truth, to recognize himself as the perfect child of God, and to live by the divine law of life.

Anything which does not measure up to the Christ pattern of perfection can be changed. Anything which the idea of God-Mind, expressing in the mind of man, has not produced can be dissolved into the original nothingness, by the understanding application of the power of spiritual thought and the resultant spiritual action.

There is nothing in the cell structure of the so-called cancer that will not respond readily to the radiations of love, life, and substance. The appearance is but the effect of concentrating attention upon negative beliefs and undesirable conditions.

Too much power has been given to adverse things, and hence too much blood has been "poisoned" and thrown into the tense part of the body in the effort to relieve it. The nature of cancer indicates some secret or unconscious resentment or bitterness toward something to which power has been attributed. The appearance shows that one has been outwardly sweet and submissive but inwardly grieved, hurt, or intolerant. Sometimes the condition we call cancer may be caused by unwise living habits, too. Whatever the cause, we know that the change in consciousness and in living habits which the Truth reveals will relieve, renew, restore, and make one entirely free.

We must agree that the doctors judge by appearance, founding their opinions upon the study of effects and drawing their conclusions from the outworking of mistakes which the individuals have made and continue to make.

No one who has awakened spiritually and is seeing his threefold being in the light of Truth speaks of disease as something of itself. He does not think for a moment that the mind is fixed in old race beliefs or errors, or that his body is unresponsive to Spirit. He ceases to think even of the name the doctors gave to the condition. He casts out and forgets their assumption that this condition could not be changed and done away with utterly, just as you would refuse to hold and to think of some unworthy or untrue thing you might hear spoken as you walked down the street.

Then, he begins at once to rejoice that he is an offspring of God. He declares that the Life and the Substance of his body are the perfect pattern of that life and body which are the gifts of God. These gifts are in reality inseparably one with God's own Being, the very essence of God-Life, God-Substance, and God-Intelligence. It is God's plan to have the creation express His own ideas, qualities, and being. Man's work is to become conscious of and to express in his life the true pattern and qualities of God.

We know very well that God would not create a man with imperfections, shortcomings, and diseased conditions. We know also that He would not create automatons who were without free will and the privilege of exercising their powers of sonship.

Chapter 23

HEALTH
IN THE HOME

I KNOW of no better way to assure the family circle that there may be health in the home than to give a chapter out of my own experience.

It was many years ago that the Truth of Being was first brought to my notice. There seemed to be urgent need of relief if my stay on this planet was to be prolonged. It was at the solicitation of friends, already interested, that my husband and I attended the first Truth class taught in the city (Kansas City, Missouri). I must have been fully ready for the initial lesson, for it filled and satisfied all the empty, hungry longings of my soul and heart. Human language cannot express the vastness of the possibilities I saw unrolled before me—*my* possibilities. While the routine of life went on pretty much the same, a new world opened within me. The physical claims that had been considered so serious faded away before the dawning of this new consciousness, and I found that my body temple had been literally transformed through the renewing of my mind.

This is how I made what I call my discovery: I was thinking about life. Life is everywhere—in man and in worm. "Then why does not the life in the worm make a body like man's?" I asked. Then I thought, "The worm has not as much sense as man." Ah! intelligence, as well as life, is needed to make a body. Here is the key to my discovery. Life has to be guided by intelligence in making all forms. The same law works in my own body. Life is simply a form of energy, and has to be guided and directed in man's body by his intelligence. How do we communicate intelligence? By thinking and talking, of course. Then it flashed upon me that I might talk to the life in every part of my body and have it do just what I wanted. I began to teach my body, and got marvelous results.

I told the life in my liver that it was not torpid or inert, but full of vigor and energy. I told the life in my stomach that it was not weak or inefficient, but energetic, strong, and intelligent. I told the life in my abdomen that it was no longer infested with ignorant ideas of disease, put there by myself and by doctors, but that it was all athrill with the sweet, pure, wholesome energy of God. I told my limbs that they were active and strong. I told my eyes that they did not see of themselves but that they expressed the sight of Spirit, and that they were drawing on an unlimited Source. I told them that they were young eyes, clear, bright eyes, because the light of God shone right through them. I told my heart that the pure love of Jesus Christ flowed in and out through its beatings and that all the world felt its joyous pulsation.

I went to all the life centers of my body and spoke words of Truth to them—words of strength and power. I asked their forgiveness for the foolish, ignorant course that I had pursued in the past, when I condemned them and called them weak, inefficient, and diseased. I did not become discouraged at their being slow to wake up, but kept right on, both silently and aloud, declaring the words of Truth, until the organs responded. And neither did I forget to tell them that they were free, unlimited Spirit. I told them that they were no longer in bondage to the carnal mind; that they were not corruptible flesh, but centers of life and energy omnipresent.

Then I asked the Father to forgive me for taking His life into my organism and using it so meanly. I promised Him that I would never, never again retard the free flow of that life through my mind and my body by any false word or thought; that I would always bless it and encourage it with true thoughts and words in its wise work of building up my body temple; that I would use all diligence and wisdom in telling it just what I wanted it to do.

I also saw that I was using the life of the Father in thinking thoughts and speaking words, and I became very watchful as to what I thought and said.

I did not let any worried or anxious thoughts into my mind, and I stopped speaking gossipy, frivolous, petulant, angry words. I let a little prayer go up every hour that Jesus Christ would be with me and help me to think and speak only kind, loving, true words; and I am sure that He is with me, because I am so peaceful and happy now.

I want everybody to know about this beautiful, true law, and to use it. It is not a new discovery, but when you use it and get the fruits of health and harmony it will seem new to you and you will feel that it is your own discovery.

I knew that this wonderful Truth was for all alike, and I began to make application of it in my home. My first test was on our laundress. My attention was attracted by her continual coughing. Upon inquiry I found that she had bronchitis; a little cold had given it an acute form, and she was spitting blood. It occurred to me that here was an opportunity to apply my divine remedy, and I said, "Lucy, I have found a new way to gain health, and I am going to try it on you." I turned within myself, and for the first time I gave what might be called a "treatment." Imagine my joy when I found that the effect was instantaneous. I interviewed her three weeks afterward, and she informed me that she had never coughed from the time of that treatment, and that all her throat trouble had disappeared. After that she always looked to me to remedy her physical ailments.

My next application was for my children. I had always been a very anxious, solicitous mother to our two sons, the younger of whom was a mere baby. The elder was subject to tonsillitis. The tonsils were becoming chronically enlarged, and the doctor said that nothing but removal of them would meet the requirements of the case. We took great care to keep him out of dampness and to comply with all the so-called precautions against cold. Our younger boy had a tendency toward croup. There are few mothers who do not understand the terror of being awakened in the night by a hoarse signal that portends this dreaded ailment of childhood.

With my new understanding, I started to teach my little ones that there is nothing in all God's world to fear. You may be sure that it was a delight to them to be released from the foolishness and ignorance that deny a child the freedom of contact with the elements. I shall never forget their shouts of joy as they waded around in the little pools made by the recent rainfalls, or when they got themselves well soaked by venturing out before the showers had ceased. One day, one of them, with a radiant face, greeted me on the porch, with a glad cry: "Oh, Mamma, aren't you glad you got more sense and aren't 'fraid any more to let us play and get our feet wet?" About this time, one of the neighbor boys from the window of his home looked out and saw our boys enjoying their new privileges, and wailed out to his mother, as she afterward told us, "Oh, Mamma, get Truth so we can wade and be happy like the Fillmore boys!"

I found that in gaining a victory over my fears I had lessened the liability of my children to take on old conditions. Of course, this was not all done at once. There were a good many times when there had to be a virtual battle with the habit of tonsillitis; but the attacks became lighter and farther apart, and gradually the tonsils became normal. As for the croupy boy, a few times the midnight alarm was sounded. But it was a trustful and not a fearful mother who came to the rescue; for well I knew that the battle was the Lord's, and with a few strong statements of Truth the enemy was put to rout, and my precious boy went to slumberland, breathing softly.

As I have before stated, these changes were not accomplished all at once. There has been a gradual giving way of the old, established ideas, as we have steadfastly made room for the higher order of living. Do not think that it was always a pathway of roses, or that my head was continually above the clouds. We had many trying tests, reverses of fortune, apparent loss of friends, humiliations of many kinds, and what seemed to be serious illness in the family. But through it all we held unwaveringly to the principles that we caught sight of in that first lesson, and we have proved beyond a doubt that God is a help in every time of need.

Our third boy came to us a few years after we received the Truth. My husband was a businessman at that time, but he was interested in my demonstrations in the family. During this period I never allowed a doubt or a fear to come into my mind. I lived to the best of my understanding and took great pleasure in helping others overcome their difficulties when they came to me for assistance. It was a very happy time of my experience, and when the dear baby came, he smashed into smithereens the tradition that woman must bring forth in pain and sorrow. So far as my comfort was concerned, I might have been up and about immediately after his arrival, but I refrained for a few days.

I think that I am qualified to say that health and harmony are possible in any home where either one or both of the parents make a compact with the ever-present and eternal Goodness to give loyalty for protection. Just so far as we trust and rely upon the great, invisible Giver, just so far and so surely shall we receive from the only Source of supply.

Whatever may seem the lack or need in the home, the supply is at hand. God's world is crammed full of health. If it is health you want, say so. God's universe is overflowing with unfailing Substance. Fill your heart and soul with it, and you will never know poverty any more. The great Answerer makes no mistake. We get just what we ask for.

Chapter 24

BE MADE
WHOLE

THERE IS often a profound philosophy con-
cealed in the root meaning of words. Words
are the outward expression of spiritual ideas,
and their roots are as the petrified remains of
an early spiritual science.

What is the spiritual meaning of the words
health and *to heal*? The words are from the
same root as the word *whole*. *Heal* comes
from the Saxon *helian*: to cover, to conceal,
and to be made whole. The Danish verb
heelen, to heal, is equivalent to being whole,
entire, and holy.

A state of health is a condition of wholeness, completeness, entireness. The word
holy is from the same root as the word *heal*.
Holiness and health in their root significance
are the same and are a state of wholeness. In
the New Testament, to be healed is to be
made whole, as in the passages, "Wouldest
thou be made whole?" (Jn. 5:6) and "Go thy
way; thy faith hath made thee whole" (Mk.
10:52). To be in health, to be holy, is to be

made "every whit whole." Jesus said to one of the subjects of his cure, "Behold, thou art made whole: sin no more, lest a worse thing befall thee" (Jn. 5:14).

In the system of Christ, holiness and health are joined. The one is the internal spiritual state; the other is the corresponding bodily condition. True health is a result, the outpicturing of the Christ ideas in thought, word, and act.

I consider this the secret of my success in healing: the spiritual revelation that God is in actuality our Father, the Source of our life and the Substance of our bodies. As soon as I saw this truth I realized that He who created us and who continues to sustain us is also patterning us after His own perfect Ideas— and that whatever He has created, He can restore!

It is up to you to accept your God-given perfection for yourself, put aside the past mistakes and the untrue suggestions, and fix your undivided attention upon the Creator of your inner pattern of perfection. This is the secret of success in all spiritual treatments. You must bring all of your mental attitudes, the centers of your consciousness, and even your physical structures, to this high place in Divine Mind where you see as God sees. In this spiritual viewpoint you are able to name all that is within you according to the patterns of Spirit; thus you are able to use these soul qualities to outpicture rightly their true creative possibilities.

It is well to consider prayerfully all of your living habits, to get a better understanding of their purposes and to know whether or not they are really chording with the divine law of health. You should consider whether or not you are worrying or fearing anything. Look back of the conscious mind into the realm of the subconscious, your memory, and determine whether there is anything that took place in the past that is continuing its disturbing influence through the unconscious expressions of your mind. (Much of the habit side of life is made up of these past experiences and trainings. Many things we do daily are not consciously thought out, but are the continuation of something impressed upon us long ago.)

HEALTH FOR THE CHILDREN

Chapter

25

(Quite often Myrtle Fillmore wrote to parents who sought her thoughts and prayers concerning the health of their children. This chapter is made up of two letters that Mrs. Fillmore wrote, one to a parent of a little girl and the other to a parent of a little boy.)

The Little Girl

NO MATTER WHAT took place at her birth, or before, or after, your little girl is still God's perfect child, and the pattern of her body temple has not been altered. The divine Intelligence and Power and Life and Substance and Love of God are ever within her, giving her all that is necessary to her perfect expression.

The anxiety of those near and dear to her at the time of her birth—and possibly the methods employed in helping her into the world, which no doubt resulted in the injury—shocked her nervous system and put fear into her subconsciousness (which is the

137

department of the mind directing and managing the circulation, muscular activities, digestion, and elimination). This subconscious fear and shock is no doubt responsible for her hesitancy in trying to walk and to use other members of the body, and for the spasmodic clutching at things. But whatever is responsible, the Truth of Being will clear out anything and everything which hindered her growth and perfect unfoldment and expression.

Tell her, quietly and simply, that when she was a tiny baby, coming to live with Mother, something occurred which hurt her and frightened her. Explain to her that her little baby mind couldn't then reason out just what had happened, and that the body, in its effort to protect her from further possible hurt, kept telegraphing to the various parts the message: "Be careful. Fight for your life. Cling with all your strength to this beautiful body. Don't take any chances by getting out of the sheltering love of Mother's arms." Now she is a big girl and wise, and has the knowledge that God's life and love are within and all about her and that there is nothing to fear. She must tell that beautiful body the Truth, as you do, and release it, and let it do the splendid things it has been built to do. She must teach her spine and her throat and her tongue and her lips and her arms and hands and her legs to do the wonderful things her mind wants them to do. She must direct them patiently in doing whatever she wishes done, until they learn to do it without her attention.

You, then, will have to learn a new way of dealing with her. You have formed the habit of doing everything for her. Now you will have to deliberately avoid responding to some of her wishes, and doing things for her. Call her attention to a thing, help her to get started, and then leave her to deal with her muscles and nerves in her own way. Remember, dear, the Spirit of God is in her little body temple; and it is the Spirit of God which is prompting her to grow and to unfold what He has placed within her.

Because souls adapt themselves to conditions under which they find themselves embodying, those who have some sort of handicap are likely to give way to it. In this case, your child may be hiding away, as it were, from the very things which remind her, subconsciously, of the sense of fear and harm. In this way she may be avoiding the learning of the very things she needs to know in order to accomplish.

On the other hand, the intense desire of the soul for full, free expression will make her tense and nervous until she learns to free herself in some systematic efforts at expression and use of all her members.

The Little Boy

Your little boy is God's child. God is both father and mother to him. The divine Father-Mother has created him and given him a perfect pattern for his life and placed in him intelligence with which to build a perfect body. God is also the unfailing and abundant supply of everything that is needed by the child for his Spirit, soul, and body. God has not only created him but is ever abiding in him as his very mind, life, wisdom, and substance. Isn't that a glorious thought?

Remember, now, there is nothing in that little boy's body but God—God Substance, God Life, God Intelligence, and God Love. There has been some failure to know how to rest and grow in the great love of God; some failure to obtain or to assimilate properly some of the body-building elements of food and air and sunshine; some failure to understand how to live by faith in the Good. All these things are the mistakes of God's children.

First of all, let us tell you that it makes no difference what the doctors have done or said. It makes no difference what the examination and the X-ray have shown. It makes no difference how the child may have been neglected through lack of understanding or lack of proper food supplies or right environment. The life of God is in your son, and about him; everything that is needed to make him comfortable, whole, strong, happy, and free is flowing into him and through him now and will continue to come.

Have you placed your faith in the doctors and the hospital for a sufficiently long period now? If so, forget them and turn your attention to God; study to understand His way and how to receive His help.

Don't worry because of what appears to be wrong with your boy. Just be glad and thankful that you can give him what no one else can give. You can care for him, for God has given him into your care and keeping. God is expressing through you as mother love, and as the wisdom which enables you to care for and help this little one.

In order that you may understand better how to deal with the little fellow, and help him, it is important to remember that children should have the right kinds of food, very early; and that they should take these foods regularly, in the atmosphere of peace and happiness and quiet and love that is natural to them. There are many mothers who do not know how to supply the foods their children need. There are some who do not have the freedom to choose the foods they instinctively would take to supply what is needed. There are some who do not know how to provide the things best suited to their needs. Sometimes financial difficulties cause parents to fail to provide what is needed.

This is the physical side of the cause of the trouble. Then there is the mental side: fear, which in some way gets a hold on the minds and emotions of little children. Fear keeps the stomach from properly receiving and handling foods taken, and causes a sort of poison in the system which in turn prevents some part of the body from getting its share of nourishing food elements. Fear hinders circulation, so that some undesirable materials or waste materials are not properly eliminated. Fear causes a gnawing hunger which makes the child or the grown-up eat fitfully—sometimes craving things not needed, sometimes refusing foods that are needed.

But thoughts of peace and *real* understanding love on the part of those near and dear, and careful study to determine just what is best in all ways, will do away with fear and all of its undesirable results.

Just let your whole mind and heart fill with love and peace. Take up this little fellow and tell him how much you love him and what a wonderful little man he is and how much better he is today. Tell him how his "little body helpers" are working to make him strong and well and how they will love to get the good things to eat which you are preparing for him. Most little folk readily get the idea of helping themselves when it is explained to them that their bodies are like lovely houses in which there are hundreds of little body helpers who are trained to take care of everything and are always busy doing the work God has made them to do. Tell him that these little helpers have had to hurt him at times, so that those who are taking care of him would know that something wasn't being done just right. Assure him that the little helpers don't want to hurt him, ever, and that just as soon as he begins to help them, they will stop making the *hurts*.

Chapter

26

GENERATION
AND
REGENERATION

*"No one hath ascended into heaven, but he
that descended out of heaven, even the Son of
man, who is in heaven."*

—John 3:13

IN THE DESCENT of the soul of man into form,
there must be some great purpose to work
out, else the world of manifestation is but an
idle dream.

There is little comfort to be gotten out of
our struggles with experience here, if they
count for nothing; but shown the golden purpose that links our efforts and struggles with
life's ascending spiral, we feel that we belong
above and not below, and are reconciled with
climbing.

The idea that man is the product of physical generation is an error of race ignorance.
Man's understanding that he is in reality
brought forth through the action of the mind
will restore him to the divine law under which
he will increase, multiply, and replenish the

earth according to the plan of God's creation.

According to the Bible allegory, it was not until after man separated himself from the spiritual consciousness of life that the curse fell upon generation, and pain and sorrow followed in its wake. In order to restore Adamic conditions, man must open his mind to divine inspiration and again walk and talk with God.

Jesus of Nazareth was an example of this restored companionship between God and man. So close was His conscious relationship with the spiritual Source of His being that He called the Source Father and acknowledged Him in all His thoughts, words, and works.

In ascribing Sonship and power to Jesus, the Christ, we are merely recognizing that which exists in ourselves and which can be developed only through the exercise of our spiritual consciousness.

"But," it may be asked, "did not Jesus have the advantage of a miraculous birth?" Yes and no. The mother of Jesus from childhood received spiritual thought and training. This prepared her for the bringing forth of the divine ideal of man, unhindered and unhampered by the physical limitations put upon motherhood by the race thought.

Mary perceived the true idea of life, looking beyond the traditions and ignorance of fleshly generation; and behold, the glory of the one and only Parent was acknowledged. With her mind and soul filled with the exaltation of the spiritual idea of what her child should mean to mankind, she drew upon herself the power of the Holy Spirit, and conceived the germ of the divine possibility. As Jesus is the type man, so Mary is the type mother.

Every mother must raise her thought of generation from the fleshly concept to the spiritual. This will bring forth the Christ child in her own soul and in her progeny, if she desires to be a mother after her divine ideals.

When once the ideal man is conceived in the mind as a possibility, and the requirements of the Law are complied with, the regeneration of mind and body is under way; then he who descended is no longer hampered by the thought of sinful flesh; he is glorified with the manifestation of divine substance in his body. This is the ascension of our Lord Jesus Christ into heaven.

Chapter 27

THE LAW OF SUPPLY

YOU SAY your world is not bounded like mine, with peace, friends, happiness, prosperity, love, plenty, and blessings of all kinds. How do *you* know what my world *is*? You are using your imagination in picturing my world to yourself. You are using the same imagination in bounding and picturing your own world— but see how differently you are using this wonderful formative faculty! See how differently you think of the people around you than of the people who are around me. Why, of course, the reactions are different. You help to make them so. People could not break through the boundaries you set, no matter how much they desired to. And so it seems to you that your life is hemmed in and friendless. Your world is sad because you continually think sad thoughts and speak sad words. This is breaking God's law of love and harmony and joy. You cannot feel God's presence so long as you disregard His laws.

You have some talent and capability that,

used to the glory of God and the honor of man, will bring you a rich reward. There is something that you can do better than anyone else can do it, and through the loving, efficient service you can render you will fulfill a need in the world. As you develop your inner resources and capabilities, the way is bound to open in the outer for you to "cash in" on your talents.

We'll get at the prosperity consciousness now, and develop your inner spiritual resources and teach you to use them to supply whatever need arises. When you look with your all-seeing, all-discerning eye of faith, you see God's abundance manifesting to meet every need of yours. So practice seeing with this inner eye that beholds the eternal verities of Being. The more you exercise this eye, the better you will see with it.

You would not think of closing your eyes and walking around saying that you can't see and don't know where you are going. So why close your eye of omniscience by saying, "I do not know what to do"? Repeatedly affirm that you *do* know! That is the way to make your wisdom work for you and guide you in paths of plenty.

When the way seems dark, pray for spiritual illumination and guidance, and bring all your thought-people into the light. You will become a radiant center of light, joy, and optimism. People will want to have you serve them. You will inspire success, for others will have confidence in you. Through understanding of spiritual laws you have a potential "gold mine" to develop.

Let the sayings and the works and the ways of Jesus Christ inspire you and lead you out into your field of service and expression; then you will find your efforts blessed with the real inner sense of satisfaction as well as with visible and tangible success. Jesus Christ's one desire was to glorify God and to reveal Him in the lives of His children. So He went about, speaking the Truth of Being to those He met and ministering with unending patience while they loitered at work He gave them to do. He knew how the opinions of men had been drilled into them until the light which God gave was almost lost sight of. Jesus' work was mostly a drill in bringing the minds of His students to grasp the Christ ideas of oneness with God-Mind, that they might pray to the Father in secret and so mold their own blessings and be able to radiate peace-inspiring, health-building qualities to others. When an individual awakens in the Christ Mind, he has no difficulty in keeping well and happy and busy with worthwhile things.

When we are endeavoring to listen, to understand, and to follow our divine guidance from the spiritual center of our own soul, we find that every wind that blows (whether it appears at first to be good or ill) does fill us with the spirit of plenty—because the winds are evidence of God's Ideas and Substance, and plenty is the one reality. So we may rejoice in our prosperity and use it day by day, in full assurance that it will never fail.

There was a time when my husband was sick and without funds. You would not have seen anything in that early environment and life of ours to give peace and happiness. We didn't know where we were to get our food or clothes or money to pay our debts. There was no evidence of plenty or prosperity. We didn't have anyone to pray for us or to offer sugges- tions of Truth; these things we had to find ourselves, in the heart of God. Those about us thought us more than a little "off," because we talked of God as our health and our supply.

But we got well and helped others to get well. We found that God had ways to provide for our needs. We kept on trusting and rejoic- ing in the Truth that came to us. We began to make new friends, who brought others.

I love to meditate upon Jesus' illustration of God's provision for all of us: "Consider the lilies of the field, how they grow; they toil not, neither do they spin" (Mt. 6:28). When all of humanity lives in harmony with the providing law of Being, man too will be blessed with plenty without having to toil for the necessi- ties of life. We can learn valuable lessons on every side when our minds are alert.

So get busy by using the Truth you know. Love those about you in a practical way; pay no attention to what others are doing, in so far as to make comparisons. Bring forth your own joyous world of love, friendship, beauty, and plenty. God is giving everything required to build such a world. There is within you the God-given intelligence to build such a world. Get at it!

Chapter 28

PROSPERITY IN THE HOME

"Peace be within thy walls,
And prosperity within thy palaces."
—Psalms 122:7

THERE NEED BE no poor homes. Every home can be prosperous. You can prove this by getting busy along the right lines. Every visible item of wealth in the world today can be traced to its invisible source. Food comes from grains. Grain is planted in the earth; but who sees or knows the secret quickening that touches the seed and makes it to bear a hundredfold? No one. That is all carried out in the invisible Source of things; but the result of an unseen force acting upon the grain is food for the multitude.

The physical substance which we call the earth is the visible form of the spiritual Substance that pervades all things. The grain is put into the earth; the quickening thought that runs through the spiritual universe causes the life germ to start and to take hold of the physical substance that nourishes it.

The word is the seed. The word is dropped into the spiritual Substance. It germinates. It grows. It brings forth after its kind. "Do men gather grapes of thorns, or figs of thistles?" (Mt. 7:16)

You who farm, and you who garden, choose the seed for next year's planting from the finest specimens of this year's crop. You reject every defective seed that you detect. If you think that your own harvest does not give you the right seed for the coming planting, you send out for the best to be had. In this way you make sure of the nature of your coming crop.

If you want prosperity in your home, you will have to exercise the same intelligent discrimination in selecting your word seed that the farmer uses in selecting his seed.

When you talk and talk "hard times," you are sowing "hard times" seed. By the sure law of growth and yield, what kind of harvest will you reap? If a farmer sowed thistle seed, and then complained that his field did not yield him wheat, you would say: "The foolish man! If he wanted wheat, why didn't he sow wheat?"

You can begin now to bring prosperity into your home. The first thing for you to do is to discard the words that have in them the idea of poverty, and then select carefully the words that hold the idea of plenty. Never make an assertion, no matter how true it may look on the surface, that you do not want continued or reproduced in your home. Do not say that money is scarce; the very statement of such a thought will send money fleeing from your fingers. Never say that times are hard with you; these words will tighten your purse strings until Omnipotence will be powerless to loosen them.

Begin right now to talk plenty, think plenty, give thanks for plenty.

The spiritual Substance out of which visible wealth comes is never depleted. It is right with you all the time. It will respond to your faith in it. It will yield according to your demands upon it. It is never affected by your ignorant talk about hard times, but you are affected because your ideas govern your demonstration. The unfailing resource is always willing to give. It has no choice in the matter; it must give, for that is its nature. Pour your living words of faith into Substance, and you will be prospered though all the banks in the world shut their doors. Turn the energy of your thought upon "plenty ideas," and you will have plenty, no matter what people about you are saying.

Another thing: You are not to take your prosperity as a matter of fact. You are to be as deeply grateful for every demonstration as you would be for some unexpected treasure poured into your lap. You are to expect prosperity because you are keeping the law, and you are to give thanks for every blessing that you gain. This will keep your heart fresh. Thanksgiving for good may be likened to the rain that falls upon the ready soil, refreshing vegetation and increasing the productiveness of the soil. When Jesus Christ had only a little supply from which to feed a multitude, He gave thanks for what He had, and that little grew into such an abundance that all were satisfied, and much was left over.

Blessing has not lost its power since the time when Jesus Christ used it. Try it and prove its efficacy. The same power of multiplication is within it. Praise and thanksgiving have within them the quickening spiritual power that produces growth and increase.

Never condemn anything in your home. If you want new articles of furniture or clothing to take the place of those which may be at the point of giving out, do not talk about what you have as being old or shabby. Watch your ideas; see yourself clothed as befits a child of the King, and your house furnished as pleases your ideals. Use the patience, the wisdom, and the assiduity that the farmer employs in his planting and cultivating, and your crop will be as sure as his.

The truths that are here spoken are energized by the living Spirit. Your mind and heart are now open and receptive to the ideas that will inspire you with the understanding of the potency of your own thought and word. You are prospered. Your home has become a magnet, drawing to it all good from the unfailing, inexhaustible reservoir of supply. Your increase comes through your righteousness.

Chapter 29

PARENTS AND CHILDREN

IT IS TRULY WONDERFUL to have children and to be truly awake in caring for them, that they may grow up in health and poise and assurance that they are God's and that all things needful come through them and to them. Parents are but representing the divine Father-Mother in receiving and caring for these new body temples which souls are building for experiences and further development of the God-given faculties and powers. Remembering this takes away the sense of anxiety and burden, and gives great peace and joy and consciousness of power and love and prosperity.

The first five or six years of an individual's life are very important, and to keep him healthy and happy and busy with suitable entertainment and work during that period means everything. He is truly laying his foundation and preparing his many faculties for the heavy school work and other activities which are to follow.

A parent should turn his entire attention to God and earnestly seek to see as He sees. The parent should see his children as eager growing souls. He should see them as individuals, unfolding their own faculties and powers, individually doing that which seems to them best at the moment. He should let his mind rise to the heights, where he can view life on a larger scale—seeing these souls not bound by convention and others' opinions and their own immediate personal problems, but as sons of God, learning by experience, by yearning, and by inspiration the way of Truth in life. He should forget the present in the eternal, and rejoice that his children have come to know God's plan of life. They are in God's kingdom—free, free to live life as they see it. They are free to change, where they feel they have made mistakes, or where the present mode of living seems to depress or to hinder progress. They are free to stand for their highest ideals, assured of blessings from others.

Lack is a word you should not try to define or even think about. Erase it from your mind because it is a seed thought that will work out in your affairs according to its kind.

Thrift consists in using wisely and to the best advantage all the resources of mind, soul, and body, as well as manifest supply. One should use wisdom in all things. One may be thrifty in using a million dollars as well as in using one dollar.

Life is a glorious experience when one keeps free from the negative and untrue and undesirable thoughts and feelings. Is it not wonderful to know that man's soul is now in tune with God's love, peace, and life and that in Truth his body need not wear out, his organs need not suffer, and he need never lack anything?

Parents and their children can do without fine homes, good furniture, cars, and the many luxuries that have grown to be a habit with many. But all of them do need one thing every day: a time for quiet prayer.

Righteousness is not a church form or moral code, but the actual application every moment of the rules of Truth which give us freedom, authority, wisdom, happiness, and plenty of the good things for the present day. The good that manifests for us is simply the result of the action of our own good thoughts and faith—without any personal effort outwardly.

Sometimes the Spirit of wisdom and love will prompt you to do things which you cannot reason out and which might seem to you unprofitable. But when you are keeping yourself in touch with God and really trusting and seeking to do the divine will, you will find all things working together for your good and the good of your family.

Divine order will be expressed in your

work when you have faith in God. Your hours will be filled with good, profitable work. You will find opportunity to encourage and help those whom the Father may send, and in this way, you see, you will be keeping your part of the universal law of prosperity and opening the channels through which your greater good will come.

Chapter 30

YOUR
LIVING SERVICE

THERE ARE no square pegs in round holes. You are where you are because there is a need to be supplied, perhaps in the way of lessons in the positive development of the faculties that will enable you to get out of the present place into a more desirable one. If it seems to you that you are a square peg in a round hole, make yourself fit into the hole you are in, or else get into another one. Don't stay there, rattling around and getting nowhere.

Your work, as you no doubt realize, is not for the purpose of supplying your own physical needs. These are supplied as gifts from the Father. Work, of whatever nature, is to render living service, in obedience to the law of giving and receiving. For you, it is for the purpose of expressing your God-given faculties and powers, to the end that you may manifest the divine ideas God has implanted, the perfect pattern of His Son.

Our work is our means of expressing what God is unfolding through us. And if our work does not do that, we are failures, even though we may keep money pouring in. The sooner we recognize that we are falling short, and make changes, the better. God is ever with us, taking care of our needs, while we are making adjustments. God momently provides what is needed. Our part is to recognize that we *are* getting what we need, and to rest in the assurance that when we are ready for something different it will come.

Heretofore you may have recognized and developed and made use of only a few of your talents. There may come a time when there seems to be no particular need for one of these talents, yet you feel that you should cling to this one avenue of expression and use it as a channel of service and supply. Don't you realize that if permitted to do so you would go on indefinitely, doing the one thing and failing to make practical use of your other talents, other ways of serving? While you might continue to sell your service and even save some money you would be poor so far as well rounded expression is concerned.

Surely you don't want to stay in the same rut always! Aren't you willing to let the Spirit of God in you draw you out in different phases of expression and development? You have accustomed yourself to certain ways and acts and returns, and you don't want to be shaken out of these habits. But it would appear that Spirit has taken a hand and is insisting that you look a little deeper into this storehouse of Mind and Substance and Love, and launch out in a different course of action and service and growth.

Consider, honestly and impersonally, just what there is greatest need of, where you are or elsewhere, and then ask the Father to help you to get into that line of expression and service. Give thanks that He is prospering you and providing for your needs.

Do not try to do too much; leave something for God to do. The Lord will bring good to pass in ways that you may least expect, when you let go and rest in the assurance that the Divine Law is working mightily. It is not necessary to "labor" for Him and "work hard" in the good cause. Just set the Law into operation through the power of the Word, and let the Law work in universal ways to bless you. It is only under the material laws set up by man in material consciousness that one has to "work hard" and live by the "sweat of his brow."

So learn to relax and let go all tense, anxious, personal striving. Take life easier and let divine ideas work for you. There is nothing for you to be tense or anxious about, either in your business life or in your spiritual work. What do you think you can accomplish by being tense or anxious, or even by strenuous personal effort? It is God who does our thinking and our work—and surely He does not find it necessary to become anxious or to strain in any way to bring about that which His plans embody.

Tension and anxiety cause one to neglect oneself and to fail in doing that which is for one's health. Do not tax your mind and body beyond what they can bear. It is necessary to observe and comply diligently with the laws governing the natural man, so that perfect order and harmony may be maintained in mind, soul, and body. Your poise and health are worth more to you than anything else you can possibly gain. You must give attention to these vital things if you would do a good work and have success.

When you give yourself to God to do His work, and then assume a lot of personal responsibility and think you have to plan and provide, can you not see that you are serving two masters? The way of the world is the way of the hireling. All the Father has is yours. You do not have to work for $30 a week or for $100 a week. The Spirit of Truth reveals to you abundant Spirit Substance as the Source of your prosperity. Affirm this to be true for you. Stop holding on to the old ideas.

Your prosperity comes through you instead of to you. And if it seems not to come, that is because you have thrown up some barrier that prevents its unfoldment through your own consciousness. Only your own changed mental attitude and living habits can cause you to work with God-Mind in bringing about the transformation.

Work is salesmanship. And if you find you have a line that is *not* in demand, or for any reason is not selling, change your line. When you wish to sell to folks, you must offer what they truly want and are willing to take and pay for. This may not always suit your personality—but then, it isn't your personality that is to be considered first. Did you ever think of that? Then do it now! Just put yourself and your accomplishments aside. Offer what is left to humanity and be determined to give the best service that has ever been given. Something will open up, something that will prove an opportunity and a needed avenue of expression, something that will renew you and give you a new angle on life, something that will clear the way for real prosperity and congenial work.

Chapter 31

THE GOSPEL
OF USES

THE HOME should be regarded as a most important factor in national life, and home-making as a sacred and distinguished trust in which all are alike vitally responsible.

Since "the hand that rocks the cradle . . . rules the world," why should ambition look farther for a mighty opportunity?

To you who are homemakers it is given to make or break the destinies of nations, since out of your homes proceeds the quality of your nation. Would you have a country ruled by love and justice? Then establish such rule in your own home. Anarchy and strife, war and bloodshed are but the outcome of inharmonious and unhappy homes.

Blessed indeed is he whose life breathes forth the harmony of a happy home. There is nothing to fear from such a one. The soul of our nation will be delivered from the "spoilers" when homes like these are in the majority. Channing might have had such a possibility in mind when he referred to "Home, the nursery of the infinite."

Could homemakers, then, ask for a greater field in which to express their aspiration and desires, to do and accomplish something great and good? Why beat your restless ambition against the bars of worry and drudgery when the opportunity and material are given you out of which to construct governments and nations that shall rise and call you blessed?

We all think that if we had certain things or were in a certain environment we would be happy. It is our privilege to have these things in order and in abundance, and it is our privilege to have the ideal environment. We have the things and the environment now; it is the use of the present possessions and the present surroundings that makes the difference between the opulent, happy life and the poor, wretched existence.

The ideal is not attained by looking afar; it is developed by a daily use of the privileges that are at hand. "Thy ideal is in thyself; thy impediment, too, is in thyself." The ideal is the thing that would satisfy the longing; the impediment is the habit of looking to the beyond for what the present offers.

In every home a certain amount of force is employed, sufficient to set and keep the household in harmony; it is able to bring into the home the things necessary for the welfare of each member of the family. The union of harmony with supply insures the ideal condition.

We must learn to use aright the power that brings what we want. Temper is power going in the wrong direction; worry and fret are exhausting misuse of the energy that should be applied to household duties. All friction in the home results from using the forces of the home along wrong lines. This is particularly true of irritability in children, who often in this way reflect the discords of others.

There is such a world of blessings at our command that our most important lesson is to know how to apply them. It is not the things that we have or that we think we need, but how we use them that tells in the life. Lying at hand, in every household, are all things necessary for the needs of the day. Adaptability will bring forth wonders. Instead of praying for more, let us ask for wisdom to use what we already have. We shall find that we are now much richer in all ways than we had thought.

Many of the irksome cares of the mother can be lessened, and finally transformed into delights. The little ones who have demanded so much in the way of attention, care, and amusement can be directed into ways of helpfulness to the mother and self-sufficiency in their own lives. It is just as amusing to the little girl to play at the game of putting the room in order as it is for her to sit by the hour engaged in some objectless entertainment. It gives the boy the right start to the right sort of manhood to know that he is able to use his strength in helping others. The little folk can, through wisdom and tact, be taught how to perform helpful acts to one another that will save the mother many a step. This method will also reduce the possibility of disagreements to a minimum. Where peace is, there is no loss of strength through mental strain. The energy that is wasted through friction in many homes is sufficient to do all the work of the household.

"But," you may object, "one cannot do all this alone, and I do not have the support of the other members of the family. Oh, if my dear one only believed in this beautiful Truth, how happy we could be!" Now, remember that if God has given you a light that your dear ones do not care to walk by, He has given it to you that you may make it so clear, so all-revealing, that it will become an illumination in the home. Not by throwing affirmations at the family, not by preaching, not through the assumption of superiority, do you recommend the higher thing. Do the thing and the thing will testify of itself.

One in a household can inaugurate all good, just by beginning and keeping it up. Pour in the oil of joy and the strength of wisdom. Utilize the blessings. Keep asking for wisdom and go on exercising what you have.

Live the joy of your new ideals in order that you may recommend them to the others in the home. Everything will fall into line, because right is the power that adjusts all forces, and one faithful member of a family can and will redeem a whole home. One joyful presence in a home will drive out every grumble. One peaceful presence will clear the house of discord. One presence of content will banish the specter of unrest. "For unto every one that hath shall be given" (Mt. 25:29). To the one who has joy shall be added joy; to the one who has peace shall be added peace.

It is joy to realize that there is a panacea for every ill that enters the home circle; and that every homemaker may hold the key that locks her doors against discord and disease. By recognizing Spirit as the source and origin of all, we may deal successfully with our problems and demonstrate harmony in the home.

Every home takes on the quality of the prevailing thought held in it; this being true, it is up to the mistress, whose thought and touch are part and parcel of the home, to look well to the manner of her thinking.

Since thoughts are things, give to your thought the quality of substance that shall embody the divine idea for which home and its furnishings stand. This is what has been called "spiritual housekeeping," and it is our privilege to carry it into all the details of the home. In the preparation of food, the mother is given the blessed opportunity of transmuting it into the very bread of heaven through her loving thought and willing service.

There can be no such thing as drudgery when housework is considered as an opportunity to make manifest some new good to her household.

You can even glorify washday by putting into it the idea of purification, so that not only the family linen comes forth clean and spotless but family affairs are made to share this weekly ablution, through the cleansing thoughts that have wrought along with the busy hand.

So each day, duty may become a joy for her who carries along with her work the idea of its spiritual significance, by keeping her thought busied with the Substance while her hand deals with the symbol.

Ironing day suggests smoothing out mental worries and creasing cares. Cleaning day and baking day have also their inner significance which will be made clear to her who seeks to carry on her spiritual housekeeping along with the work of her hands.

To deal with things divested of the vitalizing ideas back of them is feeding on husks, and productive of the weariness and discontent experienced by those who work solely in the external.

Our minds must have scope and thought

Substance. Our soul power is starved out through material methods; a knowledge of the all-providing Substance of Spirit must be ours before we are liberated from our bondage to material conditions.

Bear this statement in mind; it will help you to realization:

The all-providing Substance of Spirit is everywhere present. I mold it with my thoughts and make it tangible with my faith.

Now let us start anew, knowing that the Father has given into our keeping all the possibilities that understanding grasps. Our blessings are so great and so many that there is no emptiness anywhere in us. If we wish to do noble things we can do them where we are; if we wish to become great we have the opportunity to do great deeds just where we are. Living the Good, using the Good, knowing the power of the Good to make itself supreme, will transform every home—no matter what the conditions may be—into a home of righteousness, plenty, and joy.

We can never get into better conditions by simply running away from present surroundings. The present environment corresponds to the present state of soul development, and we only postpone the adjustment by trying to get away. Now is the time to begin the work of bringing harmony out of discord, and the wish for a better condition is the soul's prophecy of its own Good coming into appearance through its own faithful endeavors. The kingdom of heaven is within, and it is only through bringing its unfailing law of love to act upon every situation that we shall establish its peace in our surroundings.

Chapter 32

JUSTICE

GOD IS infinite justice.

Speak this. Think about it. Study it word by word. Pray for understanding of its real meaning.

Then identify yourself with God. Claim your inseparable oneness with God. Declare that you, then, are infinite justice; the justice of God is your action in all ways.

As you study this statement, you will realize that it is true that one of the qualities of God as divine law is infinite justice, ever active, throughout the universe.

You will come to understand that because you are the offspring of God, with freedom of choice, and with command of the power, faculties, and qualities of Being, you can determine just what will come into your life. You can determine what infinite justice will mete out to you. You can determine what your own attitude and acts toward others will bring to you as the result of their impressions of what you give forth.

JUSTICE

Because God is infinite justice, you can always change the causes you set into operation, and so change the results. It is always measured to you as you yourself measure by your attitude and acts.

33 | THANKSGIVING

THANKSGIVING AND GRATITUDE are qualities of the soul too little understood and exercised. Heaven and earth listen and respond to the soul that is quickened into praise and thanksgiving. Praise is gratitude in action. Try it in *your* home.

If giving thanks has in the past increased meager supply into superabundance, the thing can be done again. Elisha did it. Jesus did it. The same power is latent in you. Why not bring it forth?

If you have never practiced daily thanksgiving in your home, you have left unused one of the most potent factors available to you for bringing about ideal conditions in your household.

The mother mind and heart is the matrix in which character is molded, and home influences do much to shape the power of a nation. Given wise and loving mothers, orderly and harmonious homes, we could eventually dispense with primitive laws and corrective outlays.

A grateful, loving heart at the head of the house redeems it from discord and discontent, and ultimately changes the spears and swords of a nation into plowshares and pruning hooks.

The day of national thanksgiving is a day originally instituted in recognition of God as the Source of the nation's supply and prosperity, a day set apart as a special tribute of praise and gratitude to the great Giver of all good. Since the home is the bulwark of the nation, the responsibility of the proper observance of this holiday rests with those in the homes.

As we have reformed our method of celebrating the Fourth of July by eliminating its destructive elements, shall we not also eliminate our intemperate custom of keeping Thanksgiving with too much eating and drinking? Let us keep the spirit of thanksgiving uppermost in the home through the daily exercise of it.

Truth is freeing us from all the limitations by which we thought we were bound. We do not have to be sick. We do not have to endure unpleasant experiences. If we dwell in the secret place of the Most High, the guardianship of Truth is about us and the angels will bear us up so that we shall not dash our feet against a stone. If we would get into the habit of thinking truly about our food before we eat it, thinking where our food comes from, and then thinking back of that to Spirit, the great life that makes our vegetables and our fruits grow, there would come into our minds great praise when we ate. This praise would give new values to our food and make it taste better. Man shall not live by bread alone, but by the words of God.

Since responsibility for the proper cultivation of the appetite rests in the home, every mother should see to it that her table is provided with plain and wholesome food for the children who are forming habits of appetite that shall become permanent factors in health and soul development. It is a recognized fact that the quality of the food effects the quality of the eater. Meats stimulate the senses. Highly seasoned foods, tea, coffee, and alcoholic beverages excite the passions and appetites.

The mother's prayer for the purity and protection of her family must begin at the family table, and enter into every detail of her home ministry. She must see to it that intelligence and cleanliness of thought and practice are kept inviolate through the recognition of Christ as the head of her house.

The mother who prepares the way of her daily ministry through prayer and thanksgiving that the dear Lord is with her, and goes before her and orders the way of her household, will always be assured of the love and confidence of her family. The very walls of her dwelling shall be in league with her thoughts of praise and thanksgiving, and "holiness unto the Lord shall be written on her pots and kettles."

Since the mother gives character to the home, and the home to the nation, let every homemaker who reads this unite in making every Thanksgiving a paean of praise and a song of joy to the great Giver of our good.

Chapter 34

CHRISTMAS

CHRISTMAS! What a thrill of joy pulsates in the heart of the Christian world when the year comes around to the time in which heaven and earth lent their highest to usher in the crowning event in the progress of mankind.

The Babe born in Bethlehem was a gift to the whole world. Though the Hebrew seers had foretold, and the instructors of Israel had fixed the expectation and hope of the Jews upon the deliverer, yet Judea slept when He of whom the Scriptures testified was born. Judea slept, but the Magi from the east, the watching shepherds, and the angels gave welcome to the Christ.

Christmas! The word includes in its significance all the joys and possibilities of the God-man. Christmas is the time when angels and men rejoiced together over the coming of the Prince of Peace. The spirit of the season quickened the soul of mankind before the Hebrew prophecies were spoken.

On Christmas the sun starts on his journey northward, and the life forces within the earth feel the thrill of his radiant beams. The waiting energies of growth push out and upward, and beneath the cold and the snow, unheralded save to the heart of man, the spring is born.

All tribes and nations of earth have their legends concerning a Christmastide. In the fullness of time the dim impulse that reached out and up, groping its way to the light, found its fulfillment in the Christ-man. What wonder that heaven and earth were stirred to anthems of joy at the coming of man into his own!

Would it not be well for us to consider individually and collectively the question of how we can observe Christmas in the spirit of its true idea? We have enslaved ourselves with the burden of giving at Christmas. We have lost sight of the *real* spirit of giving when we spend ourselves and deplete our purses for the sake of conforming to the almost universal custom of exchanging gifts with our friends. It would be much more in conformity with the Christ Spirit to use the time in sending out to our friends the joyful thoughts that come spontaneously from the Christ love. The gift is but the symbol of what we desire for our friends.

When we identify ourselves with the outside things, the giving is empty and hollow; our friends do not receive much from such gifts, and neither do we. "The gift without the giver is bare."

It is the true spirit of Christmas that we should cultivate in the home. It is not the number or the value of the gifts that makes our little ones happy. Everything depends upon the interest and livingness with which the children enter into the keeping of Christmas.

Should we still tell the children the legend of Santa Claus? Every holiday season is for the purpose of emphasizing some trait in life, and it is natural that a continued observance of the season should develop the idea of a ruling genius. Christmas is the celebration of unselfishness, and giving expresses unselfishness; therefore it was inevitable that the Christmas idea should focus on a patron of childhood, some character who should stand for the providing love that delights in making the little ones glad.

Nothing could be more marvelous—and more unbelievable to the literal minded—than the Bible account of the birth of Jesus. The star, the angels singing, the shepherds, the wise men traveling from afar—all in homage to a babe born in a manger! Fairy tales? Not at all. We believe the whole account, because we know that the Christ comes not by sense testimony; we know that He comes as a spiritual, invisible Presence, and that the imaging power of the mind must necessarily build up figures by which to convey the idea of His coming within.

Because we know that every gift of the Father has its invisible source in Him, we feel that the idea of the Christmas time should be enlarged rather than diminished. We must get away from the belief that our good comes through laborious effort. We must come to know that all our supply is from the free bounty of God.

We can learn a most important lesson from the faith of the child who hangs his stockings by the fireplace for Santa Claus to fill with the gifts he has been asked to place in it. Instead of trying to lessen the faith of the child in the unseen helper, it would be vastly beneficial to us if we learned from him how to ask, stretch forth the empty hand, and find it filled.

Of course, it is not necessary to lay stress upon the Santa Claus personality. The teaching should be that there is a loving Helper who answers our prayers, an ever-ready Provider for all our needs. Gradually the teaching can lead the child more and more to understand that every good thing comes from the Father, but always faith and willingness to receive are the conditions under which our prayers are brought into visible answer.

Let us get out of the habit of thinking and teaching that life is only that which we can see, feel, touch, taste, or smell. Let us enlarge life by acting on the truth that it is "not of works, that no man should glory" (Eph. 2:9). Our children are wise in the faith that he who asks receives, and their teaching should be that which will bring them into the living reality of the invisible Supplier.

Chapter 35

New Year Opportunities

THE VERY WORD *new* gives a welcome, because there is something in the make-up of mankind that craves the freshness that the word suggests. So why not give the word *new* a place every day? Why not on first awaking remind ourselves that this is a fresh new day, full of opportunities and fragrant with possibilities? God did not endow us with brain, soul, and spirit only to have us get entangled in the web of habit.

The restrictions of yesterday have no power to overshadow our lives today, when we realize that we are in the eternal now. Let us begin our day with newness of thought and courage. Let us at the beginning of the new year throw the doors of our hearts and homes open to the *new*. The "newing" process comes first in mind. "Be ye transformed by the renewing of your mind" (Rom. 12:2).

Carry this into every detail of your life. Begin with the years and scatter them first. See yourself new, fresh, and full of vigor.

Then by the same process of transforming change everything you have to deal with daily. That which was irksome and stale now takes on a new, fresh delight.

The children of the homes are the ones who really understand the law of the new. By the touch of their untainted imagination the simplest things are transformed into the beautiful and marvelous. If we would consider this we would see that it is not the things themselves, but the thought back of them that gives them significance. The poet says, "Thou seest no beauty save thou make it first."

Beauty and appreciation are inborn, and so are all the qualities that make for the transformation in the outer world. Emerson teaches that those who have capacity to appreciate beautiful things have more enduring title to them than those who hold material ownership of them.

With this clue, who need lack possessions? The new thing to do is to let the Seer within look with unblurred vision. Michelangelo beheld an angel where the outer eyes saw only a block of marble, and with the cunning of chisel and mallet he brought into manifestation what his inner vision had created.

Looking with this inner sight we behold the angel of the new, where to the outer eyes there is mere common condition, or common experience, and the new comes forth into manifestation through the telling strokes of our thought and word.

Do you want to make new every day of the year? Have you looked on the dark side? Find the silver lining of your own ideals. Have you the habit of holding grievances? Look within and see the joy tucked away in the remote corners of your heart, and the world without will grow roseate to your charmed vision.

Go step by step through the old habits of mind and bring forth the glory of their hidden side. You will find angels of overlooked opportunities coming forth from the commonest demands of everyday life.

So ready is this glory to come into your life that you need only turn your face upon it to behold the angel of the new. Your home and life and all therein will be transformed through renewed purpose, thought, and word.

MEDITATIONS

Command of the Spirit

Stand by the Truth, for its seed is in itself.
Be the light, health, substance, beauty, and
youth of your world.
For ignorance, see light;
for sickness, health;
for want, plenty;
for ugliness, beauty;
for old age, youth;
for bondage, freedom.
Get on fire with this doctrine; let it be your
first, last, and only thought.
Our God is a consuming fire.
The righteous shall shine as the sun.
Appearances are nothing to Spirit.
Set the mind free from ideas of lust and
deception. This is freedom to heal.
No man hides iniquity.
Believe in the honesty of all people.
Like the child, see good in all things.
Distrust makes wrinkles and old age.

Keep to your intention.
Spirit fulfills your obligations.
Reiteration of Truth trains the mind.
Demonstrate prosperity. We have already
      perceived. His will is done. We do
      not beg, for it is so.
Persistence in Truth brings healing and
      prosperity.
All is Truth.

Universal Freedom

To enjoy without possession;
To see without coveting;
To have without holding;
To be without seeming;
In short, to be myself, without desiring—
      knowing that all that is, is for me,
      for my pleasure and the satisfaction
      of my immortal soul.
To say,
      "I am monarch of all I survey.
      My right there is none to dispute."
To be generous-hearted: What I see, others
      may see; what I enjoy others may share
      also on equal terms with me.

The Search

Dear Lord of my being, alone with Thee I am asking: "What am I? Who am I? Where am I?"

The answer comes from within:

"I am not what I seem. Flesh and blood do not reveal me to myself."

Back of personal estimate comes the consciousness that I am inseparably joined with Thee, and until my union is acknowledged and consummated through divine cooperation of Spirit, soul, and body, I am not content nor at one with Thee in consciousness.

"I AM that I AM."

"I am thine all possibility."

Where I am in reality is in Thy bosom. Where I am in the world of effects depends upon what I think I am.

Lord of my Being, I would be disentangled from the servitude and vicissitudes of the formed world. I would do all Thou wouldst have me do. I would be "in the world but not of it." I would dwell in the gloriousness of Thine omnipresent companionship. I would always be still enough to hear Thy voice instead of the confusion and clamor of senses. I would know and not assume. I would truly live and not exist.

Give me, dear Lord, Thy conscious support and let me be filled with the love and zeal that give character and direction to the activities of mind and body.

"I in them, and thou in me, that they may be perfected into one."

None Beside Thee

Holy One, I would do Thy will; I would give all that I am, all that I am capable of being, into Thy keeping. I would think Thy thoughts after Thee. I would give my life in making manifest Thy will in all my words and work. I would be dependent on Thee alone for my inspiration and incentive. I would know and acknowledge no other source. Thou has sent me into the world; Thou only canst direct and vitalize my effort. Help me to realize this momently: There is none beside Thee.

I Bless You

I am not deceived by appearances. You are Spirit and you are Truth. I do not believe that anyone hides iniquity, nor do you. I do not distrust my fellow men, nor do you.

You are not filled with the spirit of condemnation; you do not willfully regard appearances. You see the true Substance. You are love itself and your pure love takes in all the world.

You love Truth for Truth's own sake. Truth sets you free from pain. Truth opens your ears to hear, Truth makes you willing to do.

You are Almighty God's useful and prosperous child. I bid you go in peace. In Jesus' name you are healed. Amen.

Chapter

37

MYRTLE FILLMORE TALKS ABOUT HER LIFE

(Many persons asked Myrtle Fillmore about her personal life and background. She answered these inquiries in several letters, which we have pieced together in order to offer a brief autobiography.)

YOU ASKED ME to tell you about myself! My, I have been here so many summers that if I once opened up and began telling you the happy and interesting experiences I have had, I would soon have a little book written!

My family for generations had been members of the church. They were God-fearing people. So I was carefully reared in a Christian atmosphere. But I found that my dear ones did not have an understanding of God, who ruled in their lives, that satisfied me.

My mother was a very spiritual woman. She always kept the principles of right and love before us by her own example. She accepted the church creed and had such a devotional spirit that she felt that if her God saw fit to punish, or to do any of the many things that were attributed to God, He must have a reason for it and it was all right. I have marveled that my wonderful mother, who loved so devotedly, could have worshiped a God who punished, or took the lives of His children.

I remember my school days, and my eagerness to read and learn what others knew. I always wanted to read the books that were supposed to be for big boys, and the grownups; but little girls were not encouraged to do such reading, so I had to take my brother's books quietly and go secretly to a little corner to enjoy them. I have never been able to understand why the folks felt those books were unsuited to my eager mind. Why, they told of wonderful things, and they opened my mind until I could think things which I have been all these years fully understanding and harmonizing with the life we live day by day!

I liked the old myths, the fairy tales, histories, and scientific works. I have found that those stories, and the visions of scientists of those days and of hundreds of years ago, all have to do with our present-day life. We are discovering that the writers of myths were becoming aware of the power of the human soul, and of the ways in which we train and develop those powers. I also liked to read books which in symbol and allegory I have since learned were efforts of the authors to picture the experiences of the human soul. Then, I dearly loved the poets and I liked to write rhymes.

I delighted in getting out in the garden, or walking in the woods. I loved to touch a tree, and felt that it was truly intelligent. I received something very satisfying from my close contact with nature. I know now that I was feeling and responding to the omnipresent Spirit of God. The abundant life of God was pouring out to me from everywhere, and my hungry soul and body were drinking it and rejoicing to express it.

During my childhood there was no real understanding of God as the health of His people. So I did not know how to disconnect myself from the hereditary thought of weakness. Some of the members of my family had been weak, and some succumbed to the belief in disease. Because I was a bit different, some of them no doubt began expecting me to show signs of weakness. So I may not have had what a child should have to enable him to develop a sturdy body.

I continued to be happy with my books, my lessons, and the lovely things of the outdoors. I went on with my studies which led me to teaching school. I was not any older than some of my pupils; and I was looked upon by some of the parents of those pupils as a "girl," and they were not at all sure that they wished their big boys to go to a "girl" teacher. I smiled, down inside; for I always could see the funny side to things. I felt sure that I understood boys well enough to get along with them—and I did. We had wonderful times in those schools. I wish I had the time to tell you about them.

My first school was 'way down South. A small school was arranged for me. The building was on a battlefield. It was not so long after the Civil War, and the parents of those children had been in the war. I had to live in the homes of some of the children and had a wonderful opportunity to learn the differences in the ways of living—for many of the Southern customs were very unlike those of the Northeastern states.

Well, after several schools, and the wonderful years of coming in close touch with the many boys and girls and their parents, Mr. Fillmore came along. He was the man who was destined to catch the spiritual vision with me. When he saw me, he decided that he was going to have me for his companion. Of course, he had not yet consulted me, but apparently I did not have much to say about it! He was awfully nice, and I suppose I was a little hungry to have a home of my own, and my very own boys to help as I would like to do. And so, we were married. But I kept on with my studies, and my love for the beautiful and the things of wisdom increased. Owing to lack of understanding of the health law, neither of us was as strong as we should have been to manage a home and rear children. I suffered, the children suffered, and the burdens affected Mr. Fillmore's health, which had never been really good. And yet, when my boys came they opened a wonderful new life. We had such good times together.

All this while, I kept feeling that there was a way of life which would be discovered that would insure happiness, health, and plenty. We had an opportunity to investigate spiritual science. My receptive mind and heart kept me catching at the idea, which appealed to my reason and my intuition. After a while I was convinced that God would not create a world in which sickness, sorrow, and lack had a part.

I knew that God, whom I could call Father, would not create imperfect children. As I thought of it, I began to realize that I was truly God's child, and that because of this I must of necessity inherit from Him. Then, because the very Spirit of God is in man, I began to wake up, and the Spirit began to illumine my consciousness, and I saw that the life that is in us is the life of God. Therefore, I reasoned, the plan of God must be an inherent part of the mind of man. Since I had learned to live in books, and with the trees, I began to live with God, and to talk with Him just as I had talked with these familiar things about me.

God revealed to me that my body was intelligent; that I could direct it and praise it, and it would respond. I just assumed that God was hearing me and answering my prayers. He was giving me His Life, Substance, and Intelligence, and I was to use them, even more freely than I had used the blessings my earthly father had given me.

I did not get entirely well and strong all at once. There were a few times, after my first discoveries and healings, when I felt the need of holding on tight.

There was one time, when the household duties fell upon me with the small children to care for. I felt the old familiar heaviness, pain, the smothering in chest and the aching all through the body which meant pneumonia. I do not know why I felt that I should throw myself into the housecleaning with all the strength I could muster. But that is just what I did. I went upstairs, swept room after room; I rearranged and set in order all that part of the house, with windows wide open and perspiration flowing. I noted that I began to feel relaxed, and to breathe easier. I kept holding that God, my Father, was my health and strength. The result was that I did not have pneumonia. (However, I am not advising that others take this as a suggestion in the treatment of such appearances!)

Along with the tubercular trouble in my lungs, I had disorders through the abdominal

197

walls. At times, hemorrhoids made life miserable for me. Because this abdominal trouble had a definite cause in the realm of my own mental attitudes, it was necessary for me to grow in understanding and to make definite changes to bring about the healing. The trouble did not respond to ordinary faith and prayer. I finally asked the Lord just why it was that I did not get well. I explained that I had gone all through my consciousness to see what it was that held me, and that I had tried to find the fault.

The Spirit said to me, "You have looked among your faults; now look among your virtues." I thought that strange, but soon it came to me that I had tried to keep my feelings to myself, taking great pride in the fact that I never let anyone know just how I felt when anything displeased me or hurt me. I found that I did not feel as sweet and poised on the inside as I seemed outwardly. I began to watch, and to redeem this state of mind. I determined to handle all that came to me, before I "swallowed it" and allowed it to irritate, cut, and weaken my nerves and organs. As I gained real poise, and the ability to keep my thoughts and feelings truly free, I was healed and restored to strength and normal functioning.

I will say that in those early days, I hardly knew just what was taking place as the healings were accomplished. I only know that my experience was much like that of the blind man whom Jesus healed: "One thing I know, that, whereas I was blind, now I see" (Jn. 9:25).

I simply had great faith that God, the loving Father, had marvelously revealed Himself to me as my help in every need, and my faith inspired others to have faith. "Faith is the substance of things hoped for, the evidence of things not seen" (Heb. 11:1 KJV).

There were family problems, too. We were a sickly lot, and came to the place where we were unable to provide for our children. In the midst of all this gloom, we kept looking for the way out, which we felt sure would be revealed. It was! The Light of God revealed to us (the thought came to me first) that life is of God, and we are inseparably one with the Source; that we inherit from the divine and perfect Father. What that revelation did to me was not at first apparent to the senses. But it held my mind up above negation, and I began to claim my birthright and to act as though I believed myself the child of God, filled with His life. I gained in health and understanding. Others saw that there was something new in me and asked me to share it. I did. Others were healed and began to study.

My husband continued his business, and at first took little interest in what I was doing. After a time, however, he too became absorbed in the study of Truth. Then we consecrated ourselves to the Lord, and kept doing daily that which we felt led to do. We began to prosper, a little at a time, and our health continued to improve. Life became sweeter and more interesting, and we began to see a new world. In all these years our interest has not lagged, and we have continued to enjoy the unfoldment of God's plan in our lives.

I was always glad to pray for those who sought my help. I do not think that the success of the prayers was due to their word formations. Sometimes I merely assured those who came that I believed God could and would help them. At that time, healing seemed the most important thing in life to me. I loved seeing folks get well and happy. I do yet; but I have learned that the spiritual awakening and the daily development of Christ powers are more important. The soul must be awakened and brought to a realization of the Truth, and encouraged in the righteous use of all the God-given faculties and powers. The individual must be helped to unify his Spirit, soul, and body, in harmonious spiritual living here and now. Health is a result—the outpicturing of Christ ideas in thought, word, and act.

INDEX

opinions, of others, 83
opportunities, 185-187
order, 47, 159-160
organism, 117, 128
others, blessing, 68; influence of, 63-64; opinions
of, 83
overcoming, 103

parents, 157-160
passions, 60, 178
pattern, perfect, 9, 110,
125
Paul, 39
peace, 90
Philistines, 92
physics, law of, 30
physiologists, 118
plan, of God, 6
Plato, 39, 43
pleasure, 88-89
plenty, 148, 154
poverty, 153
power, 12-13, 22
praise, 155
prayer, 18, 51, 74, 87
prejudices, 35
Principle, 19-20
problems, reason for, 11,
20-21, 76
prosperity, 71, 148, 152-
156, 164-165
providing, 72, 150
purgatory, 65
purity, 80
purpose, 6-7, 51

race beliefs, 15
real, 30, 32-33, 66, 81;
man, 57
reality, 79
reason, pure, 22, 30-31
re-embodiment, 113
regeneration, 144-146

relaxing, 163
religion and science, 21-22
renewal, body, 17, 104,
116
restlessness, 12, 95
restoration, 117
rheumatism, 38
righteousness, 13, 32, 159
right place, 161
rut, 162

sacrifice, 89-90
salesmanship, 165
salvation, 53
Santa Claus, 182-184
satisfaction, 13, 22, 24, 61,
64, 108
science and religion, 22
science, saving, 25-28
science, spiritual, 20-21, 57
secret place, 87
seeds, 74, 85, 88
Self, real, 81
selfishness, 19
senses, 119, 121-122; closing door on, 87; five, 45;
reports of, 50
sensuous man, 33
separation, from God, 19
service, 161-165
shock, 137-138
sickness, 25-26, 30
signs, 28, 79
silence, the, 18, 74, 85-86,
88-89
sin, 25-26, 69
Solomon, 42
son-of-God consciousness,
53
sorrow, 48, 51
soul, 8, 13, 73-74, 85; and
body, 16-17, 101, 106,
109, 111, 113; home of,
43; unusual, 96-97

Further Reading

If you would like to learn more about the life of Myrtle Fillmore, her beliefs, or the origins of Unity, the following books are recommended:

Christian Healing by Charles Fillmore

God a Present Help by H. Emilie Cady

How I Used Truth by H. Emilie Cady

Lessons in Truth by H. Emilie Cady

Myrtle Fillmore: Mother of Unity by Thomas E. Witherspoon

Myrtle Fillmore's Healing Letters compiled by Frances W. Foulks

The Story of Unity by James Dillet Freeman

To purchase any of these books, call your local Unity church or center or call the Customer Service Department at Unity Village, Missouri: (816) 251-3580 or 1-800-669-0282.

About the Author

Myrtle Fillmore and her husband Charles were the founders of the Unity movement and Silent Unity, the prayer ministry that reaches around the world and publishes the *Daily Word* magazine.

Mrs. Fillmore was born on August 6, 1845, in Pagetown, Ohio, as Mary Caroline Page, the eighth of nine children. She died on October 6, 1931, at Unity Village, Missouri. Her life and work have left an impact on the world that is still being felt and will be for centuries to come, perhaps forever.

From an early age, the little girl affectionally known as Myrtle by her father, was afflicted with tuberculosis. In the spring of 1886, married to Charles Fillmore and raising two young sons, Myrtle was told that she had only a short time to live. While attending a lecture that spring, she heard a sentence that illumined the very depths of her soul: "I am a child of God and therefore I do not inherit sickness." With this Truth as a last ray of hope, she began to study and live this Truth. Over the course of the next two years, Myrtle was healed completely, having a third son in 1889 and living to the age of eighty-six.

As friends and neighbors came to her with questions and healing needs, Myrtle shared her experiences and her prayers. The prayer ministry that was to become Silent Unity and the foundation of the Unity movement was born.

For forty years Myrtle worked to experience and share "the higher vision of living—the development of soul qualities which make life a beautiful and helpful experience," planting the vital Truth seeds of Unity. These seeds of Truth have built a worldwide organization that continues Myrtle's work today, Unity School of Christianity. Unity School is a beacon of spiritual light to the world and to millions of individuals around the world through its various ministries of prayer, publishing, and education—all based on the teachings and Truth discovered and practiced by Myrtle and Charles Fillmore.

Printed U.S.A.   19-6091-75C-4-94